CREATURES OF THE BAY

CREATURES OF THE BAY

Christopher Reynolds

ANDRE DEUTSCH

First published 1974 by
André Deutsch Limited
105 Great Russell Street, London WC1

Copyright © 1974 by Christopher Reynolds

Filmset and Printed Offset Litho in Great Britain by
Cox & Wyman Ltd, London, Fakenham and Reading

ISBN 0 233 96534 3

Contents

WINTER

Left arm of the Bay seen from the cliff top.

Chapter 1

The bay lies at the bottom of the avenue in which I live. If I walk down the avenue from my home I come to a stretch of short grass where local people exercise their dogs. The far end of this grass area is fenced off with concrete posts and strong netting. It forms the top of the cliff which drops sheer down to the sandy rim of the bay. The cliff face is white because it is composed of chalk rock.

If the tide is out when I look over the cliff, I see beyond the sand a wide, flat area of seaweed-covered rock extending a hundred and fifty yards or so to sea. This expanse of rock forms the surface of the same chalk bedrock as the cliff. Once it stood high above the water, joining the rest of the land, but in the course of ages the wind, rain, frost and sea wore back the upper rock, breaking and crumbling it away, bit by bit.

The cliff curves to form a wide crescent. If I look down from the cliff when the tide is up I see no sign of the rocks, for the sea has risen above them. It covers the base of the cliff at each end of the crescent, leaving only a sandy beach within its curve. Scattered on this beach are many rounded chalk stones that gleam whitely against the sand. Some had weathered from the cliff face and fallen as boulders. These were gradually smashed and worn down by the sea. Others have been broken away and washed up from lower levels of the shore.

These chalk stones are not the only white shapes that I see from the cliff top, for there are nearly always herring-gulls in or above the bay. At low tide I see them probing for food among the seaweed-covered rocks. At high tide they paddle at the edge of the water and look for washed up morsels, or rest in small groups on the sand. Others sit

Herring-gulls rocking on the water.

peacefully on the sea, rocking like little boats as they wait for the tide to retreat. Other, more restless gulls flap and glide above the bay. I look down on their soft grey, black-tipped wings, and pure white heads and tails, as they pass below where I stand on the cliff top.

But I like best to watch the herring-gulls when there is a strong wind blowing from the sea. Then they hang at different heights above the cliff. I look up and see them as dark, outspread shapes against the grey, racing sky. The wind blows past them, quivering the feather-tips of their long wings, but does not blow them backwards. The gulls hang almost motionless, on still wings, all facing out to sea. Now and then I see them tilt and swerve as they adjust to sudden gusts or changes in the wind. Then I see one of the gulls slip sideways in a smooth, magnificent sweep that carries it above the cliff a hundred yards away. Another seagull follows. A third shoots inland, carried by the wind, then turns in a fast, wide curve. Powered by the speed of its inland flight, this gull glides forward without a single wing beat, to hold a new position above the cliff.

8

I never tire of watching the grace and beauty of the herring-gulls as they manoeuvre upon the forces of the wind. The loud rich clamour of their calls forms part of the wild music of the bay.

Herring-gulls in the wind.

Chapter 2

At the end of the short grass area a flight of steps leads down to a wide beach beyond the left arm of the bay. I go down these steps but when I reach the sand I stop, for at the sea margin is a flock of thirty small birds with longish, slender bills. They are sanderlings, pale grey above and white below, in their winter plumage – for the month is December. They run along the edge of the water and, as each wave recedes, they dash into the shallow backflow and dibble the sand with their slim bills. As the next wave returns the sanderlings retreat upshore and run along the sand on whirring legs, like little mechanical toys. Then down they dart into the backflow of the wave, to jab the sand in another hurried burst of feeding movements.

I step out on to the beach and the sanderlings rise and fly out to sea, slashing the air with sharp knife-thrusts of their pointed wings. They do not fly far, but swirl inland and settle on the shore some fifty yards away.

Sanderlings are winter visitors to the coasts of Britain. They get their name because, when not on their breeding grounds, they find their food on sandy beaches. They are, so to speak, specialists in obtaining food from this particular region of the shore. By the time they leave our beaches in late spring, their small bodies will be plump with stored energy in the form of fat.

Sanderlings breed in the Arctic Tundra, where they stay for the short six weeks or so of summer. There, each mated couple scrapes a nest in the ground. They rear their young while the tundra blooms with dainty Arctic flowers and hums with insects. Part of the stored energy, enabling the sanderlings to make the long journey to their

Sanderlings.

northern breeding grounds is produced on this very shore, in the form of little creatures caught in the backwash of the waves.

In this country we only know the sanderlings as silvery-grey, white-cheeked, white-bellied birds – but when they reach the Arctic Tundra they will have assumed their breeding plumage, with brown backs, heads and throats patterned with darker mottlings.

Visiting shore birds and gulls are constantly taking away food from the bay, but the sea is continually renewing the supply. Each tide brings nourishment to hosts of small creatures living among the rocks and in the sand, enabling them to grow and multiply. Many of these, in turn, become food for birds and larger creatures of the sea. Another portion of the life the sea produces is cast up on the beach and stranded as the tide recedes.

As I walk past the jutting cliff edge into the bay I see these stranded life-forms. Here are the dead and dying seaweeds that have lost their battle with the waves. They make a dark, curving line along the beach where the last high tide had dropped them. Seaweeds do not have roots and cannot grow in the sand. They cling to the surface of rocks by means of suckers known as holdfasts.

Chief among the seaweeds of the strand line are the brown and olive wracks that blacken as they dry. These are the seaweeds which cover most of the rocky shore. They hang, like locks of wet hair, from the mounds and ledges of its bumpy surface when the tide is low. Among the wracks I find some beautiful red seaweeds. Most of these are mossy

Stranded Red Seaweed.

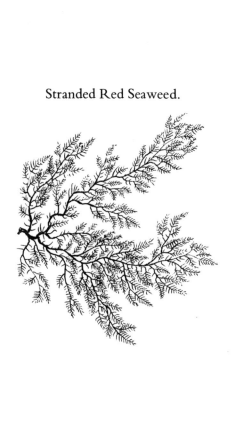

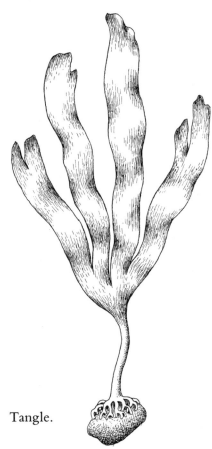

Tangle.

or feather-like, with delicate filigrees of finely divided branches. Then there are the large kelps, or tangles, strewn about. These have leathery, strap-like fronds, very slippery to the touch. Each tangle is attached by its thick, pliant stem to a broken bit of chalk stone, firmly clasped by its branching holdfast.

The tangles grow in the lowest region of the shore and on the sea-bed rocks beyond it, for they are unable to stand much exposure to the air. When the tide is out I sometimes go down and watch the projecting portions of their fronds tossing, swirling, and writhing in the restless water. Their slimy surfaces and pliant stems make it difficult for the waves to grip them and tear them from their moorings.

The general dark colour of the strand line is broken up by masses of straw-pale hornwrack. This has branching, broad-lobed fronds that fan flatly outwards and are four to five inches long. I pick up a clump of hornwrack and find that its fronds have a velvety feel when I stroke them between my fingers.

Although it looks like a seaweed, hornwrack is not even a plant. It is a colony of very minute animals whose outer cases are all joined up.

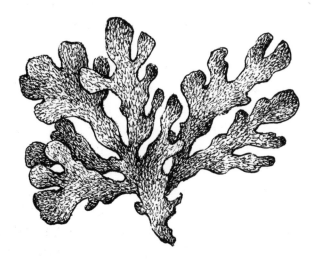

Hornwrack.

13

I take out my pocket lens and look through it at part of a hornwrack frond. Now I can see the tiny, box-like compartments, each joined by its wall to the next. There must be thousands of these box-skeletons in a single frond, and each contained a separate living animal with a circle of tentacles at the top. When feeding, these tentacles were protruded from the box to filter microscopic prey from the sea. Now the creatures have all died. A dark speck in the bottom of some compartments is all that is left of their remains.

Hornwracks grow attached to the rocks beyond the shore. They belong to a particular Phylum, or division of the animal kingdom, known as Polyzoa, which means 'many animals'. An appropriate name, for nearly all polyzoans form colonies composed of hundreds or thousands of tiny individual creatures.

Here and there along the strand line I find curious, black and rather glossy objects. Each is about three inches long, roughly rectangular, with four slightly curved prongs, one extending from each corner. As a small boy I used to wonder what these mysterious objects could be, for I often found them on the beach when we visited the sea-side. I was told they were mermaids' purses, but as I knew there were no such things as mermaids this information was not helpful. It seemed obvious to me that they were the remains of some living thing, but I could not imagine what. Now I know that these strange objects are the egg-cases of skates. I even have a photograph of a baby skate emerging from its egg-case in one of my books at home.

I pick up an egg-case from the strand line. It is very light, being filled with air, and I can find no sign of an opening through which the little skate emerged. The horny skins of the upper and under sides are joined at their ends in a narrow strip between the prongs. I try moving apart the skins, first at one end, then the other, but find I cannot do so. Fortunately I have my penknife with me. As the baby skate was able to push its way out at one end, the blade of my knife should do the same. I jab my penknife into the egg-case and push it up between the

Skate's Egg Case.

prongs. Here the blade meets a line of resistance and does not come out. I turn the egg-case round and push the blade between the prongs at the other end. It slips out easily between them.

I have discovered the front end of the egg-case through which the baby skate emerged. Now I notice that the two ends are not quite alike. The edges of the case curve inwards for about half an inch behind the front-end prongs, and the prongs themselves are slightly longer and more curved than those at the back.

There are other egg-cases scattered on the strand line of the bay. These are not single, but joined together in round, yellowish-white clumps the size of my fist or larger. They look rather like coarse, pale copies of the bathroom sponge that I used to wash down with as a child. They are the empty egg-clusters of the common whelk. The whelk is a large sea-snail, and its whitish or rusty coloured shells, up to four inches long, and often partly broken, are common objects of the beach.

I pick up an egg-cluster and squeeze it. When I stop it springs back to its original size like a sponge. The egg-cases or capsules that compose it are disc shaped, with a parchment-like skin. They are joined at their edges, but have spaces here and there between them and between the layers. This would allow sea water to circulate through the clump so that the developing young could breathe.

15

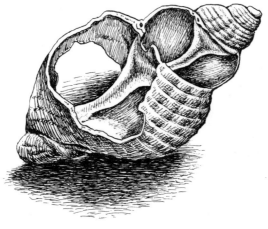

Egg Cluster of Whelk.

Broken Whelk shell.

I count the egg-capsules on part of the clump, and estimate that there are about three hundred on the whole surface, and perhaps twice that number inside. The female whelk turns round and round while laying her eggs so that the sticky masses build up to form the rounded cluster. The egg-clusters are fixed to stones and rocks down beyond the shore. Soon after the baby whelks have crawled out of their capsules the cluster breaks free and gets washed up on the shore.

Now the raw, wintery air is stinging my wet hands and making my fingers numb. I shall soon be down again, for one never knows, from one week to the next, what interesting life-forms may be thrown up by the sea.

If you remember to wrap up well and avoid lingering too long in one spot, the strand line can provide a constant source of interest through the winter months, when it is far too cold to go dabbling in the rock pools and the sea. There will be plenty of opportunity to do that later in the year, and then you will be able to take your shoes off and paddle at the same time – and even search for creatures while you bathe when the summer sun has really warmed the water.

Chapter 3

It is a brilliant late December morning. Not a cloud flecks the blue void of sky which fades to mist above the sea's horizon. Left of the far shore and the shaded cliff, the surface of the incoming tide shimmers with dazzling sun-flakes. A redshank probes the hollow of a nearby pool and then stands still. Against the dark wrack strands its legs and their reflections gleam like sticks of red fire in the morning sunlight. I move

Redshank in a sandy pool.

four steps down the beach and the redshank shoots up and flies away, twice uttering its plaintive, three-note call – 'tew-we-wee, tew-we-wee'. Beyond where the redshank stood some herring-gulls walk about on the brown and glittering seaweed-covered rocks. I hear a curlew and watch it fly over the outermost rocks, its curved bill barely visible.

Just inshore from the rocks, and right across the bay, the sand is dotted with myriads of small hummocks. They stand out darkly against the sand's wet, sun-bright surface. These hummocks are the coiled casts of lugworms and are composed of sand and mud that has passed through the bodies of the worms. Each tide brings a fresh supply of food for the lugworms, for the sea abounds in microscopic life. When the tide retreats, a portion of this gets left behind and washed into the sand, together with fine morsels of decayed seaweed

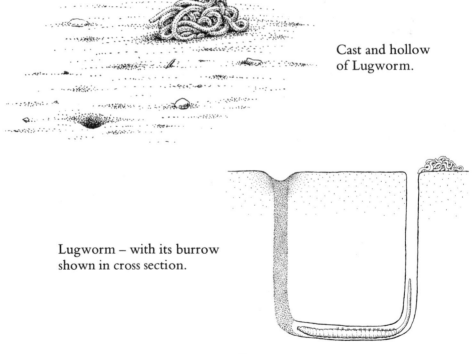

Cast and hollow of Lugworm.

Lugworm – with its burrow shown in cross section.

and other debris. It is this organic matter – we call it 'organic' because it is derived from living organisms – that the worms digest from the sand and mud they swallow.

Four or five inches from some of the worm casts, I notice a little cup-shaped hollow in the sand. This lies over the head-end of the lugworm's burrow. The lugworm lives in an L-shaped burrow. Its head thrusts up into the blind end at the toe of the L as it works the sand and swallows some of it. This activity causes a continuous downward movement of sand from above its head, leaving the little hollow on the surface where debris and tiny organisms collect. These gradually move down and enrich the sand which the worm swallows.

When a lugworm is ready to void the waste sand from its intestine, it wriggles backwards up the vertical arm of the L until its hind-end is at the surface. The waste sand comes quickly out, like tooth-paste being squeezed from a tube, to form a coiled worm cast on the sand. When the tide has just gone down and swept the sand clear, I like to watch these little mounds of coiling sand suddenly appear, one after another, above the lugworms' burrows.

Now I go over and make several rough counts of the worm casts. From these I estimate that there are, on average, about twenty lugworms to each square yard of this region of the beach. Having settled this I walk with yard-long steps over the stretch of lugworm casts and find that it takes two hundred and seventy strides to cover it. As this band of worm casts extends in width for several yards upshore, I reckon there must be about thirty thousand lugworms in this portion of the bay. Many thousands more live in the sandy gaps and channels between the rocks. A considerable amount of sand and mud must pass through the bodies of all these lugworms every day. This helps to keep the organic content of the sand in proper balance, and without their aid the shore would tend to become foul.

Below the belt of lugworm casts, and in the shelter of the rocks, I notice signs of another worm that lives in the sand. The signs are like

Tube of the Sand Mason Worm.

little chimneys that rise an inch or two from the surface. These chimneys are hollow tubes built of sand grains and bits of gravel, and each has a frill of sandy threads at the top. With my fingers, I carefully poke away several inches of surrounding sand from some of the tubes, and find that they continue down below. These are the tubes of the sand mason worms, so called because they build their homes of sand and gravel.

When the tide comes up and covers its tube, the sand mason, if undisturbed, pushes its head out and spreads the thread-like tentacles that surround its mouth. These feeding tentacles are used to sweep up organic debris and minute life-forms from the surface of the sand. The sand mason also uses its tentacles to pick up sand grains and gravel for making or repairing its tubular home.

Here, on this small stretch of shore, are the obvious signs of two worms with very different feeding habits. The first is a sand swallower, extracting organic matter from the sand grains underground. The second is a deposit feeder, using its tentacles to sift its food from the surface. But now I must go and explore the strand line.

I walk up the beach and lift a large tangle from the strand line. Its holdfast is attached to two chalk stones and a mussel shell. The mussel shell is slightly agape, so I move the two shell valves further apart and find a very small crab squatting beside the rotting remains of the mussel. The crab is still just alive. I take it carefully out of the shell to examine. It is a delicate little creature: the body, about a third of an inch across, is round, shiny and yellowish-white with rose-pink markings, and its small pincers and feeble legs are almost transparent. This is a female pea crab. It had not found its way into the mussel shell by accident, but was actually living inside before the mussel got washed up.

Pea Crab in shell of dead Mussel.

After floating in the sea as a minute larva, the baby pea crab finds its way into the shell of a living mussel. If it is a female, it spends the rest of its life there, taking part of the food that the mussel strains from the water, but doing no harm to the mussel itself. When full grown it is too plump to escape between the shell valves, which only open a little way to allow water to be drawn in. However, the much smaller male pea crab can easily do so. He wanders from mussel to mussel in search of a female to mate with.

I take the little pea crab down the beach and throw it out to sea, knowing alas, that it is most unlikely to survive. The female pea crab is adapted for squatting inside a mussel shell, and its feeble legs are quite unused to making journeys in search of a new home. Even if it does come across a mussel it will probably be unable to squeeze between the shell valves – but I have done what I can to help it.

This sort of partnership, where one kind of animal takes part of the food that is caught by a different kind, is known as commensalism, which means 'feeding at the same table'. There are many other instances of commensalism in the animal kingdom.

I pick up another mussel from the strand line. This shell is also slightly agape, so I open it wider, but find it empty. Now I push the two shell valves together between my fingers. When I release the pressure they spring slightly open. This shows that the living mussel has to use force to keep its shell valves tightly closed when danger

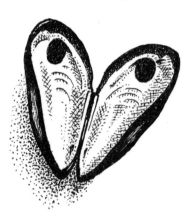

Empty Mussel Shell. Showing points where the shell-closing muscle was attached to each valve.

threatens, or when the tide goes out and leaves it exposed to the air. I open the shell valves wide and notice that they are joined near the narrow end, or beak, of the mussel, by a slightly elastic, horny hinge. This is called the ligament. It shows the position of the back of the mussel, while the two shell valves cover the left and right sides. Unlike the rough exterior, the inside of each shell valve is smooth, shiny, and almost white with a dark border and a dark circular patch near the wide end. These dark patches mark the points where the powerful muscle for closing the shell was attached to each valve.

The mussel is a Bivalve Mollusc. Molluscs are soft bodied, wet-skinned animals without legs. Most of them have a hard, limy shell which serves as an outside skeleton. The two biggest classes of Molluscs are the Gastropods, or snail-like Molluscs, which have a shell in one piece, usually with a coiled spire, and the Bivalves, where the shell is in two parts joined by a ligament.

To put it briefly, the typical Gastropod has a head bearing tentacles. It scrapes food into its mouth by means of a finely toothed tongue, called the radula, and moves about on a muscular suction pad known as the foot. The typical Bivalve has no head. It moves by means of a fleshy, finger-like foot which can be protruded from the front end, and breathes and feeds by means of two siphons which protrude from the rear of the shell. In breathing, water is drawn in through the lower siphon, passed over the gills which enfold the body organs, and expelled through the upper siphon. At the same time minute organisms and other food particles are strained off on the sticky slime, or mucus, which covers the gills. This mucus is continually drawn forward to the mouth and swallowed with the food it contains.

I look up and notice that the tide is rapidly coming in over the rocks. Now I must hurry along the beach and leave through the gap between the water and the cliff edge before the sea blocks my way.

From the cliff top I look out over the shining bay. The tide is now well up the shore and only the nearest rocks are still exposed. A flock of thirty oyster-catchers, flicking white bands on sharp, black wings, sweeps in a wide arrow-head above the sea. As the flock passes, parallel to the shore, I see its pursuing shadow skim the rippling water. On a sandy puddle beside the rocks I spot a single redshank, perhaps the one I saw before. As I watch, he gives a formal bow, then bobs his head up–down, up–down, with a curious clockwork action. He then turns left and repeats the strange performance, as if rehearsing to himself his part in some bird pantomime. Some twenty yards along the shore I just make out the squat, plump forms of three purple sandpipers moving about and probing on the rocks. Their small, dark bodies are well concealed against the wrack strands.

Purple sandpipers are closely related to sanderlings, yet the two birds have very different feeding habits. While sanderlings find their food at the water's edge on the sandy part of the beach, purple sand-pipers probe for small creatures on the seaweed-covered rocks. They only settle on the sand to rest at high tide. Thus, the two kinds of birds never make claim to the same food.

The particular feeding place of any creature is known as its 'ecological niche'. Ecology is the study of living things in relation to their natural surroundings. Any distinct, major habitat, with its special group of living things, is known as an 'ecosystem'. Thus, purple sand-pipers and sanderlings avoid food competition by occupying separate niches in the seashore ecosystem.

Purple Sandpiper.

Chapter 4

Cold easterly winds were lashing the sea into foaming waves through-out last week. Today, however, it is fairly calm, although the January air is bitter. The tide is half-way down the rocky expanse, and about twenty black-headed gulls – their heads white with only a dark mark behind the eye – are paddling at the sea's edge in a sandy gap between the rocks. Off to their right some herring-gulls are walking about on the exposed rocks, probing the seaweed with their beaks. I notice that one has caught a crab and is busily tearing it apart. Beyond the shore, three herring-gulls are resting on the water, and on the furthest rock a great black-backed gull is standing, alone and statue-still, just looking out to sea. As I move along the strand line an oyster-catcher flies up from the rocks, calling 'kleep kleep' as he hurtles away over the grey water.

Turning now to examine the strand line, I notice some new objects that the rough seas have wrenched from the rocks. These objects have from three to six rounded lobes, an inch to three inches long, arising from a fleshy base. Some are white, some yellow, some orange, and some flesh pink. They remind me of some forms of fungus that I have occasionally seen, but even more they resemble the knuckle ends of hands with stunted fingers. In fact, they bear the rather gruesome name of dead men's fingers.

I pick one up and it feels like rubber or tough jelly. Through my pocket lens, I see that its surface is pitted with small craters, and lining each crater is what looks like a little eight-rayed star with a minute hole at its centre. The star is formed by the tentacles of a creature called a polyp, and the central hole is its mouth. Each dead man's fingers is

An Oyster-catcher
flies up from the rocks.

really a colony of hundreds of tiny polyps embedded in its rubbery mass. The polyps themselves have delicate, tubular bodies, each with a mouth at the top surrounded by eight feathery tentacles.

When alive and undisturbed in the sea, a dead man's fingers looks really beautiful. The polyps extend from its surface and spread their tentacles, so that the finger-like lobes appear to be covered with tiny, delicate flowers. The tentacles are used to trap and sting minute drifting creatures which are then pushed into the mouth. All the polyps, however, are joined by tubes below the surface of the colony, so the food caught by any one polyp goes to nourish its neighbours as well.

Dead men's fingers are related to the corals that form barrier reefs in tropical seas; but unlike these huge colonies of coral polyps which are enclosed in hard, limestone skeletons, the dead men's fingers colonies have rubbery skeletons. For this reason they belong to the group of polyps known as soft corals.

Further along the strand line I notice something that looks like a small, leafless bush with fleshy branches. Soon I find some more. They are pale brown, and vary from four to eight inches in height. The short

26

main stem ends in a disc-like holdfast, and the branches fan out side-ways. I pick one up and find that the branches have a spongy texture. They squeeze flat between my fingers and regain their cylindrical shape when I release them.

What I am holding is, in fact, a sponge of a particular kind known as a branching sponge. Really it is the fibrous skeleton of a branching sponge, for the living cells of its body have died and shrivelled away. A sponge is an extremely simple kind of animal. Water, containing food and oxygen for breathing, is drawn in through minute pores in its surface and expelled through larger pores.

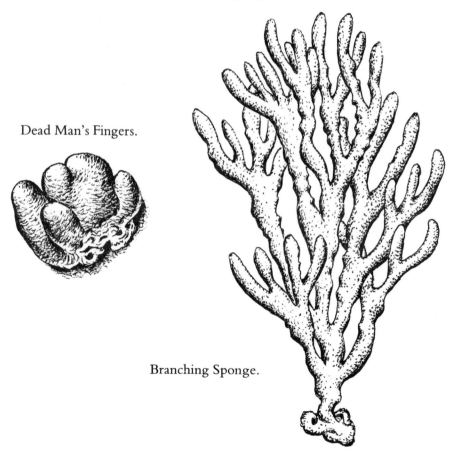

Dead Man's Fingers.

Branching Sponge.

Branching sponges live down below the shore. They flourish from ten to fifteen fathoms deep, in the dim, bluish light where tangles and other offshore seaweeds disappear. I know this because I recently saw a film on television where the photographer swam down past the sloping forest of huge tangles, and showed us the miniature forest of branching sponges which covered the rocks of this twilight world.

Sponges, corals, and hornwracks are able to take on the form of plants because their food is carried in the water that surrounds them. In the same way, the substances which nourish a tree are contained in the air that surrounds its branches and the soil that covers its roots. The main difference is that whereas such plants as trees, flowers, ferns and seaweeds are able to use the sun's energy to build their own food from simple, non-living substances, all animals must take in ready-made food in the form of animals or plants, their dead bodies, or their products. The branching sponges filter from the water the myriad microscopic particles of organic matter which drift, like invisible snowflakes, down from the surface and the rocks above.

As I walk further along the strand line my eyes are suddenly held by a white shell valve, slim and elongate, like a wing. I pick the shell valve up and see, to my delight, that it is complete and undamaged. I have found others cast up on the beach, but all have been partly broken, for these shells are very fragile. This is the left shell valve of a piddock. I look for the right shell valve, but hardly expect to find it, for the half-shells of piddocks are not hinged together by a ligament as in other Bivalve Molluscs. In any case, it would probably be broken.

I have often crushed and splintered damaged piddock shells between my fingers, yet they are the instruments by which the living molluscs bore their way into rocks. Many of the chalk stones which have been wrenched from the rocky sea-bed and then cast up on the beach, are pierced with smooth-walled holes of varying size. These holes were made by piddocks, and a few of them have parts of the shell still wedged inside to prove it.

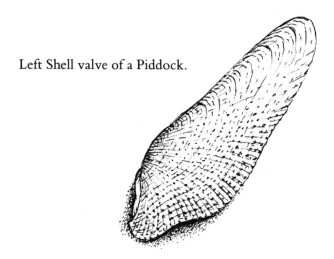

Left Shell valve of a Piddock.

I run my finger along the surface of the shell valve in my hand. The front end feels rough, like a file, but the rear portion is smoothly ridged. The roughness is due to hundreds of minute teeth which line the ridges at the front part of the shell valve. Through my pocket lens I can see these teeth quite clearly, and though the shell itself is fragile, the teeth are very hard. However, piddocks do prefer to bore into fairly soft rock, and it is because the rocks here are made of chalk that piddocks are so abundant in the bay. As they are very well protected in their holes it does not matter that their shells are fragile.

Now I examine some of the chalk stones that are pierced by piddock holes. The holes are perfectly round, but they taper slightly from one side of the stone to the other. This is because the piddocks bored their way gradually into the rock, keeping pace with their own slow growth. The eggs of piddocks hatch into tiny larvae that drift and swim in the sea. Soon they settle on the surface of a rock, grow a shell, and start boring their way in. The boring is done by the toothed surface of the front part of the shell valves, and the strong, sucker-ended foot which pulls the shell firmly to the rock base. Two powerful muscles attached to each shell valve work alternately to rotate the shell first one way and then the other. Thus it acts like a drill and makes

29

a neatly rounded hole in the rock. Again I examine my shell valve and see that the front margin is cut away in a graceful curve. This is where the thick, muscular foot projected to hold the shell down while it was rotated.

The siphons of the piddock project from the rear end of its shell. They are united to form one double tube which tapers to fit the outer narrowing of its hole. Thus the siphon tips can be extended to reach the rock surface while the piddock, deep in its close-fitting lair, peacefully filters the drifting microscopic life-forms from the sea. When the tide goes out and leaves the rocks exposed, the piddock pulls down its siphons and waits, safe from the probing bills of gulls and waders, till the food-laden waves return to cover it.

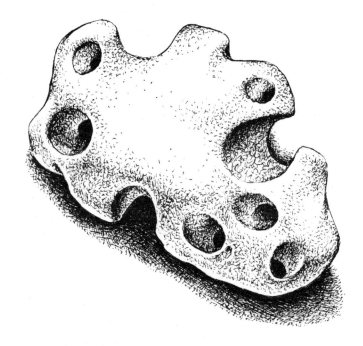

Chalk stone pierced by Piddock holes.

Chapter 5

As I look along the beach, I notice that above the main strand line, there are other smaller and drier strand lines. These were left by previous tides that rose higher up the shore. The tides do not rise to the same level every day. They are governed by the pull of the sun and the moon on the earth, but as the moon is so much nearer its pull is stronger. The largest tides, known as the 'spring tides', occur twice a month, at the time of the new moon and the full moon. At these times the flood tide comes high up the beach and the ebb tide goes far down the shore. The smallest tides, known as the 'neap tides', occur at the half moon periods, seven days after new moon and seven days after full moon. Then the distance between high and low water reaches its shortest limit.

Seaweed fly.

A few yards down shore from the lowest strand line, where the slope of the beach levels off, I notice a speckled, blue and white line of mussel shell valves and tiny chalk stones. These, being very light, but not floating, were jostled about by the backwash of the waves as the tide began to fall. When the tide reached the more level sand, the backwash was not strong enough to pull them any further and dropped them along this line.

Now I walk up the beach to the top strand line and turn over a clump of seaweed. On doing so I disturb a number of flies that were resting below; some crawl away and hide under the nearest litter, and a few fall on their backs and buzz feebly round in circles. They seem too sluggish to be capable of flight, yet it is surprising to see living flies actually moving about on this cold winter morning. They will remain below the seaweed in a dormant state until the warm spring weather comes.

These are the seaweed flies that may be seen in their thousands on the beach in summer. They run about on the strand line, and over the sand, the stones, and the limbs of sun-bathers, and make short, hopping flights from place to place. Often they crowd to feed on choice morsels dropped from the lunch packets of holiday-makers. Last summer I saw a dark circle of them clustered round a melting blob of ice-cream on the sand.

Seaweed flies lay their eggs on the strand line, and their larvae, which are yellowish maggots feed on the rotting seaweed. These maggots perform a useful service, for they act as 'decomposer organisms'. While they are feeding, the maggots partially dissolve and soften the seaweed all around them. This helps to release substances that the seaweeds had built into their bodies as they grew. These substances eventually get washed back into the sea to be re-absorbed by other seaweeds and the myriad microscopic plants that drift in with the tide. Thus, by assisting decay, the seaweed flies, with the help of sandhoppers, bacteria, and other decomposer organisms, renew the shore's fertility and encourage growth.

However there are certain objects on the strand line which do not decompose, and which did not originate in the sea; such things as cartons and plastic cups, bottles, polythene bags, torn rubber beach shoes, a garish plastic bucket, and other oddments left by holiday-makers from the summer months. These objects provide no food for decomposer organisms, and remain, as unsightly litter, defiling the natural features of the bay.

Oiled Guillemot.

I walk further along the top strand line and come across something that troubles me even more. Lying on its back is a dead guillemot, with dark spots of oil clotting the feathers of its breast and neck. Every year thousands of guillemots die as victims of oil pollution from ships at sea.

Outside the breeding season, guillemots spend the whole of their lives at sea, and rest or swim on the water when not flying above it or fishing below the surface. Then, if they do come to an oil slick, their reaction to it is their downfall. They dive, and thus make themselves even more polluted. As guillemots cannot remain under water for more than a minute, they are likely to surface in a patch of oil and get themselves in a worse state than ever. Their vain efforts to clean themselves with their bills only causes the feathers to clog together more firmly. This breaks the water-proofing of their plumage so that the sea water wets their skins, and they eventually die of cold.

Guillemots are not creatures of the bay. They live out in the deeper waters of the continental shelf, where they dive for fish, using their wings to swim with underwater. The only ones that enter the bay are those that get washed up on the beach, after suffering a cruel and miserable death of starvation and cold, while struggling hopelessly to remove the cloying filth from their bodies.

Chapter 6

It is a cold, fine February morning, and as I look down from the cliff top I see that the tide is up. Two herring-gulls rest on the beach below me, and to their left, six oyster-catchers stand together looking very smart with their sharply contrasting, black and white plumage, pink legs, and bright orange-red bills. Further along the beach about thirty sanderlings, as many turnstones, and a single redshank, are standing grouped together on the sand.

When the tide has covered the rocky expanse and the water reaches the outjutting cliffs which form the two arms of the bay, the beach becomes a refuge for gulls and many waders. They feel secure to rest on this curve of sand which is then cut off by the sea from the other beaches. When the tide goes out they disperse to various feeding grounds along the coast.

I start to walk along the cliff and the herring-gulls and oyster-catchers fly out from the bay. The herring-gulls alight and settle on the sea, but the oyster-catchers swing left and streak away, flying low above the water. I walk a few more paces and now the sanderlings and turnstones take alarm and hurtle out to sea, forming a close, mixed flock. Only the lone redshank remains standing on the beach.

I turn my eyes from the redshank and see the flock of sanderlings and turnstones fly shorewards and settle on the same part of the beach they had vacated. After walking and running here and there, the turnstones come together, settle down to rest, turn their heads round, and tuck their bills beneath the feathers of their backs. Five minutes later a flock of fifty more turnstones comes flying in from the sea. They settle beside the others, move about until they are lined up in loose, straggly ranks all facing seawards, then tuck their bills in their backs and sleep.

Meanwhile the sanderlings have started to disperse along the shore. Splitting into parties of three or four, they run back and forth along the lapping sea edge, now and then darting into the backwash to peck and jab their bills in the retreating water. There will be more food for them when the tide has ebbed a little further down the sand.

I begin to feel chilled with standing on the breezy cliff top, and as I turn from the sea I notice a flock of black-headed gulls resting at the far end of the grassy stretch. Some are standing, some sitting on the grass, but all are facing out towards the wind. In the centre of the green

Redwing.

a couple of jackdaws are probing in the turf, and quite near me three redwings are hopping and stopping, waiting alert and watchful, then hopping again, as they search the ground for hidden worms. I might have thought they were song thrushes had I not noticed the pale eyebrow stripes, and rusty-red patches on their flanks. The redwing is, in fact, a species of thrush that nests in Scandinavia and spends the winter with us.

On my left about fifty starlings move along in close formation as they hurriedly probe and prise apart the grass roots in a ceaseless quest for food. I start for home, and the starlings fly up, wheel, and settle some fifty yards to my right, but the redwings are unperturbed and merely hop away as I approach them.

An hour and a half passes, and having warmed myself thoroughly at home I make my way back to the cliff top. The tide has retreated some way down the sand, but no part of the rocky shore is yet exposed. The redshank, now accompanied by five purple sandpipers, is still resting on the beach, but only a dozen turnstones remain. Below them, and at the water's edge, about eighty sanderlings are feeding. They follow the retreating surf, peck hurriedly in the sand, then dart up-shore, inches ahead of each pursuing breaker, only to turn again and rush back into the surge. Acting together, they make a second, living tide of silvery-grey birds, pulsating back and forth with the same slow, steady rhythm as the first.

There is something very romantic about these lively little waders that nest in the high Arctic regions. They travel great distances along the shores of many countries, living always out there on the windy edges of the world, with the tumbling waves on one side and alien land on the other.

Sanderlings feeding.

Chapter 7

Days of raw, wet weather have kept me indoors, but at last the rain has cleared. On reaching the cliff top I see eight herring-gulls loosely lined up along the beach below me, for the tide is well above the rocks. The gulls look up nervously and some take a few steps towards the sea, but they do not fly. To their left, in the centre of the beach, a hundred and fifty oyster-catchers are resting, mostly on one leg, with their bills tucked in their backs. Now the solitary redshank flies in from the sea, alights behind the oyster-catchers, and immediately puts up one leg, hunches his head on his shoulders, and sleeps.

Some twenty yards beyond the oyster-catchers, fifteen black-headed gulls are resting, well up on the beach. Below them are active groups of turnstones and sanderlings. The turnstones move here and there over the sand and poke their bills into seaweed clumps as they search for sandhoppers, flies and washed-up morsels. I notice that one

Turnstones.

has found an opened mussel. He tries in vain to extract the contents, but the mussel shell slips forward from each bill-thrust that he makes. Other turnstones are paddling at the edge of the sea and pecking here and there in the foam-flecked water. The dull shade of their winter plumage is relieved by their twinkling orange-red legs, as brilliant as the oyster-catchers' bills.

Sanderling with its reflection in the wet sand.

Turnstones get their name from their habit of turning over stones with their bills in search for food, but I have not yet seen them doing this. Their main feeding grounds are out on the rocky expanse, where they poke about under seaweeds, into crevices, and down among the sand and debris between the hummocks of rock, where many small creatures lurk.

The sanderlings run incessantly along the shore and into the surf and back, hardly stopping as they deliver quick jabs in the sand or water.

39

They seem to have boundless energy, and their small black feet pat-pattering along the shore, carry them six yards in a couple of seconds. As they run by the sea edge, a yellow-brown reflection companions each silvery bird, moving below it on the shiny, surf-washed sand.

Five purple sandpipers fly in and settle in front of the oyster-catchers. Now the redshank wakes up and goes down to join the sanderlings. He struts about, seeming tall among their darting forms, and occasionally stops to prod the surf with his slender, two-inch bill. One of the herring-gulls walks over to the flock of oyster-catchers, discovers something in the sand, and lunges at the nearby birds. The

Herring-gull and Oyster-catchers.

alerted oyster-catchers sidle away leaving a vacant circle around him as he digs his bill into the sand. Now he pulls a yellowish object up and walks away, head high, with the object dangling from his beak.

I move along the cliff top to the right side of the bay, and there I see a close group of sanderlings actually resting, with bills tucked in their backs. Presently a few wake up, run down into a retreating wave, and bathe. They dip their heads, flap, splash, and shuffle their wings in the water, then dart upshore just in time to avoid being smothered by the oncoming breaker. Upshore they stop, rub their black bills up and down their breasts, and then make fluttering leaps into the air to shake the water from their wings. Then down they go for another dowsing, this time joined by three others, and the whole lively performance is repeated.

Suddenly I realise that I am shivering, and my joints stiff from the cold breeze. I had been too absorbed to notice my discomfort. Reluctantly I turn away, walk rapidly up the road and warm myself at home.

Winter is the great time for watching shore birds. It is the time when they congregate in greatest numbers on our shores. In spring they gradually disperse to their breeding grounds, and in autumn they come filtering back, some sooner and some later, according to their kind, and the distances they have had to travel. But remember to wrap up really well against the weather. Continual movement will disturb the birds, so you must be sufficiently insulated from the cold to bear standing still, or crouching in one position, for quite a time.

Two and a half hours pass and I return to the cliff. The tops of the nearest rocks are now exposed. A dozen herring-gulls are standing on the shore. They see me on the cliff top and four of them fly out to join two others floating on the sea. Ten yards beyond them a great black-backed gull rocks gently with the rhythm of the swell.

Now the eight gulls on the shore start up a clamour of calls. One after another they throw up their heads, and with open bills raised skywards, they call, 'kew, kew, quow, quow, quow, quow'. The infection spreads, and two of the floating herring-gulls point up their bills and call in answer. Then suddenly they stop, and all is peace. The oyster-catchers continue to slumber, with one leg raised and bills tucked in their backs. Sanderlings still run into the surf – turnstones probe the strand line – and at the far end of the bay, thirty black-headed gulls paddle and peck in the shallows.

Soon, the oyster-catchers begin to wake up. One after another, they lift their heads, and a few raise their wings and stretch them upwards in a kind of yawn. Some hop on one leg further down the shore, and

Herring-gull calling.

others walk down to the sea. One oyster-catcher wades up to his belly, dips his head in the water, shuffles his wings and splashes, then returns upshore. A few more follow his example, but most are content to stand on the wet sand, or step about in the shallows.

Now the herring-gulls stretch their wings and fly silently out to some newly exposed rocks beyond the right arm of the bay. The gulls on the water fly up and follow them, and all alight on the islands of

Oyster-catchers in flight.

rock well out from the shore. I hear a shrill 'klee-ip', and see an oyster-catcher flying out from the bay. It flicks on a straight course, inches above the water, and joins the gulls on the emerging islands. Another 'Klee-ip, klee-ip' sounds as two more oyster-catchers leave the bay. A few minutes later another one departs, then three, then a group of seven, then one again, and then a flock of twenty, each bird calling 'Klee-ip' as it streaks across the water. In a quarter of an hour all the hundred and fifty oyster-catchers have left the bay to hunt for food on the offshore rocks beyond it.

Soon a group of turnstones flies up from the shore and out towards

Turnstone in flight.

the rocks. A moment ago they were dumpy, short-legged birds, padding about on the beach. Now they are utterly transformed. White-rumped, with long, sharp-pointed, white-barred wings flicking the air, they hurtle, arrow-swift towards the emergent rocks, leaving their companion sanderlings to dibble in the puddles and stream-channels of the lower, rippled sand. The turnstones need to be fast and well-powered in flight, for like the sanderlings, they nest on the stony surface of high Arctic lands.

A clamour of strident squawks and raucous screams turns my attention to the left side of the bay. There the black-headed gulls are paddling, fluttering, flapping, quarrelling, and splashing in the shallows. It seems the receding tide has offered them something special in the way of food.

The black-headed gulls forage inland for food as well as on the beach and among the rocks. I see them in the meadows and ploughed fields, and they follow the ploughing tractors to pick out upturned worms from the furrows. They also join the herring-gulls in scavenging on refuse dumps along the coast. During the hard days of snow and frost last month, black-headed gulls came to feed on the crumbs thrown out for garden birds on the lawn behind my house. They were very cautious and would circle round and round before daring to swoop down to snatch a piece of bread, cheese or fat. Their light-winged, wheeling forms, circling above the garden made a wonderful aerial ballet that was a delight to watch.

The gulls and waders are the chief predators of the various molluscs, worms, crustaceans, fish and other creatures of the shore. Most of these creatures are more or less permanent inhabitants of the bay, but the gulls and waders come and go. They take their pickings from this and neighbouring shores. Some stay in the neighbourhood of the bay for weeks or months at a time. Others merely call to feed for a day or two, and then proceed on their passage along the coast.

The rocky shore of the bay is an extremely rich and productive area of living things, and the gulls and waders are, so to speak, an end result of this rich source of food. It goes to provide them with the energy they need to live, breed, and perform their wonderful feats of flight. The original source of this energy is not the living food in the bay, but the sun that gives it light and warmth.

The seaweeds of the bay and the teaming microscopic plants that drift in with every tide, trap this sunlight energy and use it to build up the material of their bodies from simple substances in the sea. They alone, of all the life-forms in the bay, can use the sun's energy. We call them the 'producer organisms' because they produce the food on which all the creatures of the bay finally depend. The animals of the bay are called the 'consumer organisms' because they consume, either directly or indirectly, the various plants.

The creatures that feed directly on the plants of the shore are called the 'primary consumers' or herbivores. The winkles and limpets that feed on the seaweed encrusting the rocks, the minute swimming animals that feed on the drifting microscopic plants, and the mussels and piddocks that filter microscopic plants from the water are primary consumers.

45

The primary consumers provide food for 'secondary consumers', or carnivores. A purple sandpiper that eats a winkle, or a starfish that eats a mussel, is a secondary consumer. When a purple sandpiper eats a winkle, it feeds indirectly on the seaweed that nourished the body of the winkle. Secondary consumers may be eaten by other carnivores called 'tertiary consumers'. A herring-gull that eats a starfish that feeds on mussels is a tertiary consumer. Here, the herring-gull eats the minute, drifting plant life of the sea at 'third hand', so to speak.

Thus, we get what is known as 'food chains', with shore birds at the head and plants at their base. A very simple food chain may be represented thus: green seaweed → winkle → purple sandpiper. This food chain has three links. The case of a herring-gull eating a starfish represents a four-link chain. It may be written thus: microscopic plants → mussel → starfish → herring-gull.

Of course, purple sandpipers do not only eat winkles. They take small fish, worms, crustaceans and other molluscs as well, and the winkle may be eaten by a redshank or a turnstone, or even by a man. Winkle pickers come into the bay at low tide from time-to-time and fill their sacks with winkles which land up in stalls or food shops of the towns.

All the interlocking food chains in the bay, together form what is called a 'food web'. The various creatures that compose this food web are in a state of natural balance. For instance, although the oyster-catchers eat mussels, the number of mussels in the bay remains fairly constant from one year to the next. The mussels themselves produce eggs which become new mussels that replace those that were eaten, but if anything happened to cause the mussels to die, then the oyster-catchers would be in serious trouble.

A chain is as strong as its weakest link, and if one link snaps, or one type of creature is destroyed, then quite different animals that relied, directly or indirectly, on that creature for food may disappear as well. This, of course, applies to any natural system of living things, whether it be a line of shore, a pond, a wood, or a mountain meadow. The destruction of one or more links in a food chain – the links may be animals or plants – is what is meant by the phrase 'upsetting the balance of Nature'. The food webs that link living things together in any natural system are very intricate and finely balanced. Thus the destruction of one link can have quite unexpected and far reaching results that may be disastrous for many creatures.

SPRING

Chapter 8

It is a brilliant mid-March afternoon, and the sea is an intense, sparkling blue. The tide is low, and the wrack-covered rocks are golden brown, wet and glistening, their colour emphasised by black areas of shadow. Some turnstones are moving about on the nearby rocks, searching among the wrack strands for small creatures. Further out are herring-gulls, pale grey and dazzling white. Some are standing, others probing the rocks for food. On the furthest rocks I spot four oyster-catchers. I see first their glowing red bills, and then their pied bodies, black as the shadowed rocks with glints of chalk stone white.

As I start to walk down a sandy channel between the rock mounds, the turnstones rise with chittering calls. Together, they streak out and away to my left, almost skimming the water. I take a few more steps down shore, and the oyster-catchers fly up and hurtle away to my right, voicing alarm at my intrusion with sharp, far-carrying cries, wild as the salt wind. Only the herring-gulls remain, standing with

Male Gammarid
carrying a female.

necks raised and alerted gaze. Some seconds later they, too, fly up and glide away.

I bend down and turn over a large chalk stone in the channel. A dozen greenish grey gammarids – their scientific name is Gammarus – scuttle away on their sides, curving and uncurving as they go. Some of the males, half an inch in length, carry smaller females curled beneath their bodies. These small crustaceans, shaped like quarter moons, and flattened from side to side, are scavengers of the mid-shore level. Now I spot a very young shore crab, with an olive green back not a quarter of an inch wide, and yellowish legs as dainty as a spider's. It crouches for a moment, then sidles rapidly to the rock edge and retreats beneath a wrack frond.

I replace the chalk stone and lift up the curtain of wrack weed that covers the side of the rock. As I do so three dark grey periwinkles fall to the ground. I pick one up and see that its shell entrance is closed by a

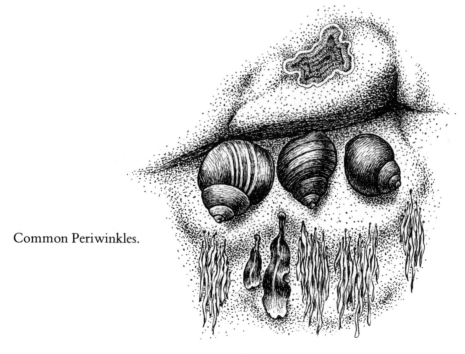

Common Periwinkles.

horny disc that fits it like a door. This is the operculum. It lies on the upper surface of the winkle's foot, at the tail end, and when the animal retracts into its shell the tail curls inward and thus shuts and seals the door. In this way the winkle conserves the moisture in its shell while it rests uncovered by the sea. If it becomes dislodged it is also protected from the prying claws of a crab, and, I should think, from the bill of a shore bird. To test this, I jab the shell opening with my pencil. Its point merely hits the operculum and does not penetrate the winkle's body. Dislodged periwinkles can be rolled and tossed about by the waves and come to no harm, for their shells are very hard.

Another periwinkle remains lightly fixed to the rock. This one is yellowish-grey, marked with thin dark bands. Below it there is a cluster of acorn barnacles. Their shells are like little ridged cones with the tops cut off to reveal an inside cap of four minute plates, tightly closed. Now a pale brown bristle-worm comes out of a crevice,

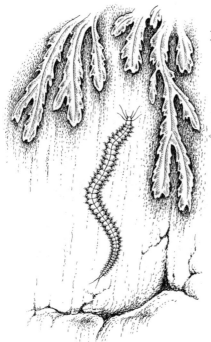

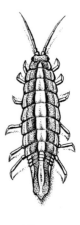

Bristle Worm crawling up the rock.

Idotea.

52

crawls up the rock, and disappears between the wrack stems. Although it is a true worm, the creature looks rather like a centipede. Its head bears two pairs of tentacles, and its body segments are flanked by bristly, leg-like projections which allow it to crawl along. The bristle-worm is carnivorous. Hidden within its mouth is a pair of pincer-like jaws. These can be shot out to capture the small creatures on which it feeds.

The side of the rock itself appears to have been painted with patches of mauve-pink. I scratch the edge of one of these coloured patches with my fingernail and reveal the white chalk surface underneath. The patches are, of course, not paint, but the living forms of an encrusting seaweed called Lithophyllum. It grows as a hard, thin film over the rocks.

On a frond of the wracks that hang over my arm, I notice a dark green creature with a pale stripe down its back. I take it carefully off the frond, and in my hand it looks like a rather narrow woodlouse, about half an inch in length. The creature has no common name. Its scientific name is Idotea, and it is, in fact, a marine relation of the woodlouse. I place the Idotea on the edge of a gravelly puddle at my feet. Immediately it swims with a fast, gliding motion and settles at the other end.

Already, without moving a step, I have found four different kinds of crustaceans – gammarids, a baby shore crab, Idotea and acorn barnacles. It may surprise you to learn that barnacles are crustaceans not molluscs, and it was only when their life history was discovered in 1830 that they were recognised as such. The minute larvae which hatch from the eggs of barnacles live a free life, swimming in the sea, and are similar to the larvae of certain other small crustaceans. Eventually, the tiny larva fixes itself by its head to the surface of a rock, changes its form, and secretes around itself the conical shell with little movable plates at the top.

When the barnacle is exposed at low tide, these plates are closed, like

53

Barnacle with
tentacle-like legs extended.

trap doors, to keep the moisture in, but when the water rises and covers it, they open, and a tuft of feathery tentacles uncurls from the top. These tentacles are really the barnacle's legs, which are used to capture microscopic organisms in the sea. Every second or so, they are suddenly withdrawn like the closing fingers of a hand, and the barnacle eats the captured organisms.

I walk slowly down shore and lift some more of the stones that litter the channel, always being careful to replace them as they were before. Under the stones are more gammarids and young shore crabs. Many of the little crabs are of a dark greenish colour, but one is rust brown. Another is almost black with a crimson mark on its back, and several bear white patches that look like tiny chalk stones. One is completely white. They are well camouflaged for living on the gravelly surface of the channel. The larger shore crabs that I find all have dark green backs, and most of them lurk under the wrack strands that border the channel.

One stone that I lift has a hard-shelled, oval creature pressed firmly to its underside. The shell is made up of segments, and the flattened rim surrounding it is so firmly pressed to the surface that the creature looks like the back of some fossil embedded in the stone. It is wonderfully adapted to survive the buffeting of the sea. Even the roughest waves could hardly dislodge it. Although the segmented shell gives it the appearance of a somewhat flattened, legless woodlouse, this

54

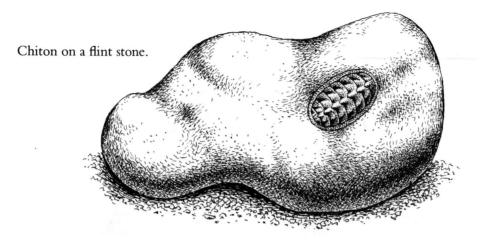

Chiton on a flint stone.

creature is, in fact, a mollusc, with a shell composed of eight jointed plates. It is called a chiton, or coat-of-mail shell.

I carefully prise the chiton off the stone with my penknife. Its under-surface is made up of a fleshy foot, like that of a snail, in front of which is a small head without tentacles. The mouth is on the underside of the head, and the chiton feeds by scraping the film of minute seaweeds from stones and rocks with its radular. I drop the chiton into a pool in the channel, and it curls itself into a loose ball, like a nearly closed pill woodlouse.

Stuck firmly to some of the flint stones are shells of quite a different kind. These are white, tubular shells, twisted like little writhing snakes. Each is the home of a worm called Pomatoceros. Unlike the sand mason worm that builds its tube from the gravel and sand around it, Pomatoceros secretes a limy shell from substances in its body, in much the same way as a mollusc does. When the water covers it, the Pomatoceros extends a ring of feathery tentacles from the mouth of its tube. These act as gills for breathing, and as a net for trapping micro-scopic organisms which are then wafted towards its mouth. One of the tentacles, however, is not used for these purposes. It is thickened towards the tip and acts as a stopper to close the mouth of the tube when the worm retreats.

Pomatoceros with tentacles extended.

I notice that whereas the Pomatoceros tubes are common on the flint stones, there are none on the much more abundant chalk stones in the channel. The eggs of Pomatoceros hatch into minute larvae that drift and swim in the sea. The larvae will only change form and become attached if they make contact with a smooth surface like that of a flint stone. They will not do so when they come against a granular surface like that of a chalk stone.

Further along I notice some more white tube-shells. These are attached to a wrack frond that overhangs a rock mound by the channel. The largest is less than an eighth of an inch across, and they are coiled like the shells of snails. These are the shells of another worm, closely related to Pomatoceros. This little worm is called Spirorbis. It also feeds by filtering microscopic organisms from the sea with its feathery tentacles.

There are some snails, too, on the wrack weeds. Their rounded shells, about half an inch across, are not easy to see. Most of them are dark, olive green, or brown to match the wrack fronds, and a few are amber or yellow like the frond-tips. These are flat periwinkles, so called because the coils that form the spire of their shells are flat, and not pointed, as in most snails. Unlike the common periwinkles which live on the rocks and scrape minute, encrusting seaweeds from the surface, flat periwinkles live and feed on the wrack fronds. One of them is crawling up a wet, shaded frond on the ledge beside me. Its head and slowly waving tentacles are bright orange, making a vivid contrast to its dark, greenish shell.

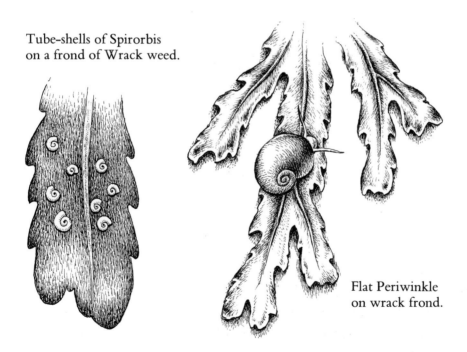

Tube-shells of Spirorbis
on a frond of Wrack weed.

Flat Periwinkle
on wrack frond.

As I return up the gravelly channel, I notice that there are two kinds of wrack weeds on the rocks. The rocks above the lowest shore levels are covered with serrated wrack. This wrack is easy to distinguish. The edges of its flat, branching fronds are jagged, with forward-pointing teeth, rather like those of a saw.

Further up the shore I see clumps of bladder wrack growing among the strands of serrated wrack. The rocks still nearer the beach are entirely covered with bladder wrack. The shorter fronds of this wrack

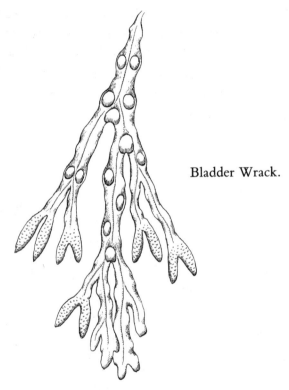

Bladder Wrack.

have smooth, rather wavy edges. But what really distinguishes it are the pairs of air-filled bladders on the fronds. It is rather fun to jump on clumps of bladder wrack and hear the bladders burst with loud 'plops'. However, the bladders were not made just for our amusement. They act as floats to buoy the seaweed up when the water covers it.

Above the area of bladder wracks, I come to the bright green rocks that border the sandy beach. These rocks have no wracks growing on them. They are covered with the thin, ribbon-like fronds of a green seaweed called Enteromorpha. So the seaweeds are not mixed up in any haphazard manner on the shore. They grow in particular zones, each species living where conditions favour its development and survival. The length of time a seaweed can endure the drying effect of wind and sun limits the zone its species is able to occupy along the shore.

. In cracks and crevices of some of these inshore wracks, there are bluish clumps of mussels. The mussels are firmly anchored to the rocks by rough, brown threads. These threads, which together form what is called the byssus, are secreted by the mussel's foot, and spread out under and around its shell like the guy ropes of a tent. The byssus anchors the mussel securely against the buffeting of the waves, yet allows it to swivel so that, if not in a tight cluster, it can face the force of the sea. In this way its streamlined form is able to resist wave action. The effectiveness of the byssus in securing the mussel is well seen further down the shore. There, the tops of some of the higher rocks, swept clean of seaweeds by the surging breakers, bear thriving colonies of mussels.

Like the piddock, the mussel filters microscopic plants and particles from the sea, but its siphons are short and do not extend much beyond the rim of its opened shell. A single mussel is able to filter the impurities and microscopic organisms from two or three pints of water an hour. This filtering ability was well demonstrated when a tank of murky sea water, containing rocks on which a number of mussels were anchored, was placed in a laboratory for some students to observe. After a few days the mussels had made the water so clean that one of the students, viewing the mussels from above, actually stuck his face in the water, thinking the tank had been emptied.

The mussels clustered on the inshore rocks are all tightly closed.

I hold one of them firmly against the rock surface without tearing it from its moorings. Then I try to prise open its two shell valves with the blade of my penknife, but find this quite impossible. The shell valve edges fit together so perfectly that the tip of my blade will not enter between them at any point. Thus the sea water that was enclosed by the mussel's shell when the tide uncovered the rocks cannot leak out or evaporate away. The delicate gills and soft body parts of the mussel will be safely bathed in the private pond its shell has trapped, until the sea returns to cover it again.

Many of the larger mussels have barnacles growing on their shells, and a few have the tube-shells of Pomatoceros worms fixed to them as well. Thus, by their very presence, the mussels provide extra living space for smaller filter feeders. Within the mussel shells, too, a special niche is provided for the little pea crabs to occupy. In the same way, the wrack weeds that hang from the rock mounds of the mid-shore levels, provide cover and a moist habitat at low tide for a host of crustaceans, worms, and molluscs that could not live exposed on the bare rock.

So the more plants and animals there are in any habitat, the greater is the number of ecological niches made possible for other forms of life to occupy. In fact, the health and beauty of any ecosystem are determined by the variety of animals and plants that it contains.

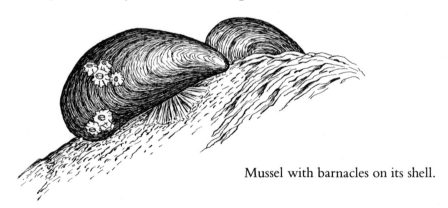

Mussel with barnacles on its shell.

Chapter 9

There are no flowering plants on the shore to mark the spring, but a pair of fulmar petrels have arrived from the north. I stand on the cliff top in the evening light, and watch them flying, one after the other, along the face of the cliff. Perhaps they are prospecting for nesting ledges or hollows in the chalk.

The fulmars are grey winged and white, like gulls with short, thick bills and large, black eyes. They fly with straight wings, not elbowed like those of a gull. On reaching the end of the bay they turn out to sea, then circle back, steep-tilting as they wheel, with wings held stiffly

Fulmar.

outwards so that one points down to the water, the other to the sky. Then up they come, first one and then the other, to the jutting arm of the bay, beating the air with shallow wing-thrusts. Again they shoot smoothly along the cliff face, flying with an easy momentum that is beautiful to watch. Again they turn out to sea and circle back to repeat their flight along the cliff – and yet again – and all the time they are strangely silent.

The light begins to fade. My eyes have followed the fulmar petrels for a quarter of an hour. Now they are flying out to sea. They do not circle back this time, but carry straight ahead and fade from view above the dim horizon.

The fulmars have departed, but their flying images stay in my mind as I stroll back towards my house, and remain with me, sharp and clear, for many hours.

The tide is low and I wander down the shore, lifting stones here and there from the gravelly channel. As I lift one large chalk stone a piddock falls out from its hole. The pounding waves had probably broken this stone away from the side of a rock mound, one rough and stormy day. Successive tides had then wedged it between two other rock mounds. Meanwhile the piddock in the stone continued to bore

Live Piddock.

its way down as it grew larger, until its tunnel reached the gravel underneath. But now I have the chance to sketch a live piddock in my note book. I place it on its back to show the sucker foot between the curving shell valves at the front, and the fleshy siphon-tube projecting from the rear.

Having now finished my quick sketch, I push the piddock deep into its tunnel, and with my fingers over the hole, heave the stone back until it is nearly down on the gravel. I give the stone a final shove, and it is again firmly wedged between the rock mounds, with the piddock secure in its home. There is time for it to recover from whatever shock it suffered before the tide comes in with a fresh supply of microscopic food.

Further down the shore I lift a curtain of wrack weed from a rock and disturb a large shore crab. The tail of this crab, instead of being tightly tucked beneath its body in the normal manner, is partly pro-

Shore Crab with Sacculina.

truding. Anxious to discover the cause of this, I catch the crab by holding it firmly with my thumb on one side of its back and two fingers on the other. This hold prevents the crab from being able to nip me with its claws. On turning it over, I see a rounded, orange lump protruding from beneath its tail. The thing looks like a kind of fungus growing out of the crab's body. Actually it is another crustacean.

Yes, Sacculina, to give it its proper name, is a parasitic crustacean, related to barnacles, that grows like a fungus. It sends a network of feeding threads into the crab's body, while a rubbery sac containing the reproductive organs and countless developing eggs, grows out from the crab's abdomen. It has no nerves or sense organs, and there is

63

little to suggest that it is even an animal, let alone, a crustacean. You might call the Sacculina a fungus barnacle. It is a perfect example of what can happen to a creature that takes up a completely parasitic life.

However, the eggs that are shed from a pore in the Sacculina's body, hatch into minute, free-swimming larvae. It is these larvae that give away its true identity, for they are similar to those of barnacles. After swimming in the sea for a short time and changing its form, a lucky Sacculina larva (if you can call it lucky), finds its way to a young crab and attaches itself. So far it has behaved like a typical barnacle larva, but from now on strange things begin to happen. The attached larva casts off its swimming legs, pierces the crab's skin, and pours the cells of its body into the crab. These cells join up beneath the crab's intestine to form a new body. This grows feeding threads which branch and spread to all parts of the crab. Meanwhile its central body expands. It finally breaks out through the moulting crab's abdomen, and develops reproductive organs.

It takes about nine months for a Sacculina to develop fully, but once this has happened, the victimised crab is unable to shed its shell, grow, mate, or lay eggs, but it may continue to live with its burden for a year or so.

Chapter 10

Although there are no flowers on the shore to spangle this April morning, the fertile frond-tips of serrated wrack, that slowly paled to amber through the winter, are now spangled with orange spots. Many are even coated with an orange slime, and where the frond-tips dangle into pools, an orange cloud drifts from them in the water. This means that the male and female wrack plants are releasing their reproductive cells.

When the tide comes up and covers the frond-tips, these microscopic cells, now held in the orange slime, will be washed into the sea. Then individual male and female cells will fuse together to form fertile eggs. Many of these eggs will be eaten by tiny creatures or filtered

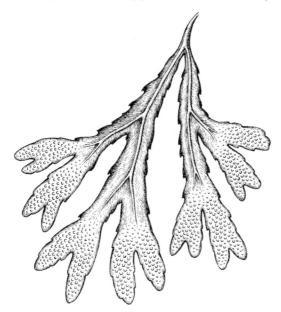

Fertile frond
of Serrated Wrack.

from the water by tube worms and bivalve molluscs. Plenty, however, will survive, attach themselves to rocks, and become new wrack plants.

These reproductive cells do not get washed straight out to sea and wasted when released, for the wrack plants have a mysterious wisdom. Their fertile fronds only extrude these sex cells at low water when the tide has begun to turn. The incoming sea, as it floods the frond-tips, then floats the cells over the rocky levels of the shore. There is time for them to meet and fuse, and for the fertile eggs to sink before the ebb tide starts surging down the beach.

I tear off a serrated wrack frond with orange slime on its tip and put it in a plastic bag to examine closely when I get home. I always take one or two polythene bags with me when I come down to the shore. They hold water so that small creatures placed in them will remain alive and seaweeds keep fresh while I carry them about. The tops of the bags can be screwed up and closed with a small elastic band.

On the rock face under the hanging wrack fronds I notice a large limpet. Its conical shell is in the centre of a cup-shaped hollow in the rock. I give the limpet a quick, hard knock with my fist to take it by surprise. This moves it back about two millimetres, but now it pulls its shell down so firmly that no amount of knocking or shoving will budge it. The limpet is obviously secure against even the strongest waves, and the conical shape of its shell, fitting perfectly to the rock, offers no grip for the water.

The limpet is a kind of Gastropod mollusc, or snail, that has no coiled spire to its shell. When the water covers it, the limpet moves out from its hollow in the rock and feeds, using its finely-toothed radula to scrape minute, encrusting algae and other small seaweeds from the surrounding surface. Any of the fertile egg cells of serrated wrack that land on this surface, and start to grow, will not survive very long.

When the limpet moves from the hollow to start feeding, it leaves a small, inner depression that exactly fits its shell. This depression, or 'limpet scar' is the limpet's home, to which it must return before the

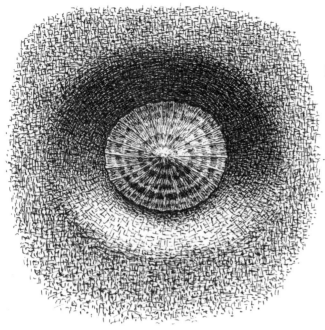

Limpet in its home.

falling tide uncovers it. The scar is caused by the abrasive pressure of the limpet's shell wearing down the rock. The cup-shaped hollow surrounding the scar must have been worn back and widened over many years, for this large limpet, with a shell-base two inches long, could well be in its teens.

On each return to its home, the limpet slowly revolves until it faces the same direction as before, then, prior to settling down, it shuffles its shell slightly until it has found the perfect fit between shell-edge and rock. Here, and only here, is the limpet safe when the sea uncovers it. There is no other resting-place that will trap the water in its shell, prevent evaporation, and save the delicate gills that surround its foot from drying. For this reason the limpet never wanders far while feeding, but keeps an area well cropped around its home.

As I come to the jutting cliff edge on my own way home, I notice a white patch of exposed chalk in the green belt of Enteromorpha that covers its base. The patch is about a foot across, and at its centre is a green lump. On coming close, I see that the lump is a limpet with Enteromorpha growing on its shell, and the white patch is its feeding area. Near the edge of the patch there is a film of green algae and tiny Enteromorpha plants. Here, I notice some white zig-zag lines where the limpet's radula has scraped the chalk surface clean.

Back home I remove a bit of orange slime from the serrated wrack with a small paint brush, and rinse it into a drop of sea water, on a microscope slide. Now I place the slide on the stage of my microscope and look through the eye-piece. I slowly turn the adjusting screw, and the drop of sea water comes into focus, presenting me with an amazing sight. Hundreds of tiny black dots are darting here and there in the water. They remind me, more than anything else, of a buzzing swarm of bees.

These tiny dots are the male reproductive cells, or sperms, showing that the frond I brought from the shore belonged to a male plant. The female reproductive cells, or eggs, are larger and do not swim. They slowly sink in the water when washed from the frond-tip, and release a substance that attracts the sperms. The sperms themselves swim through the water by lashing two whip-like hairs, called flagella, but these are much too small for me to see.

Now I examine the surface of the frond-tip. On close inspection the orange spots that cover it look like little raised pimples. I take a razor blade and cut a very thin slice through a few of the orange pimples, and place it on another slide in a drop of sea water. Under the microscope, I see that each orange pimple has an opening at the top, leading down into a circular cavity. This is called the conceptacle, and within it the sperms, or in the case of female plants, the eggs, are formed.

Each conceptacle has branching hairs, that look like tiny trees with pod-like fruits, the hairs growing from its walls. I see that most of the

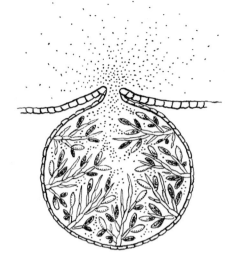

Section through male conceptacle
of Serrated Wrack showing sperm cells
escaping into the water.

(Seen under the microscope.)

pods are transparent and empty, but a few are dark and full of sperms.
Other sperms are darting about in the conceptacle, and some escape
from the opening at the top and go careering through the water drop.
Whoever would have guessed that there could be so much exciting
activity in the frond-tip of a common seaweed, when spring comes
to the shore.

The wrack weeds, with their coloured frond-tips, inform me of the
spring, but in most of the other seaweeds, some of which have extremely complex and interesting life histories, there are no very
obvious changes to mark the seasons.

Actually I picked another wrack frond to bring home before
leaving the shore. I did so because I noticed a greyish film spreading
partly over its surface. I see, through my pocket lens, that the film is
made up of thousands of minute, box-like compartments, similar to
those on the fronds of hornwrack. So this is another kind of polyzoan,
which has a different encrusting habit of growth.

The compartments of hornwrack colonies form a double layer
covering both sides of its fronds, but this polyzoan has only a single
layer spread out on the seaweed frond. It looks very beautiful under

the lens, for the whitish sides of the tiny compartments give it the appearance of fine lace, and they stream outwards with the growth of the colony, so that it almost seems to flow.

The hornwracks that I found washed up on the strand line were dead, but this colony is alive, and most of the compartments, or capsules, are occupied. I place the wrack frond, with the polyzoan facing upwards, in a small saucer of sea water and wait for things to happen. Presently I see, through my pocket lens, a silvery white brush push up from one of the capsules. Now it comes up further, half opens then

Encrusting Polyzoan
on a wrack frond.

Polyzoan colony magnified.

spreads out to form a whitish star of tentacles. I make a slight movement, and like a flash, the little animal has shot back into its capsule.

I wait patiently, not moving a muscle, with my lens focused on the colony. Soon there are scores of pale, fragile stars outspread above its surface. Every now and then, a few of the little zooids, as the individual animals are called, seem suddenly to take fright, and flash back into their capsules. Half a minute later, each cautiously pokes up its little brush, half opens it, then spreads its tiny star.

Where the seaweed frond curls over at its edge I can see some of the zooids in profile. Each crown of tentacles, hardly visible against the white of the saucer, caps a minute stem, which is the body of the zooid protruding from the open front end of its capsule. The tentacles themselves are lined with beating hairs, called cilia, which are quite invisible except under a high-power microscope. These waft minute organisms towards the zooid's mouth.

Polyzoans are also known as bryozoans, which means 'moss animals', on account of the way many of them spread over surfaces like mosses. Some zoologists use one name, some the other, so you can take your choice. They are also commonly known as sea mats.

Chapter 11

It is high tide, and as I stand on the cliff top I see below me about eighty turnstones and some fifty sanderlings all resting in a close flock on the sand. Twenty yards beyond them is another flock consisting of forty purple sandpipers and six sanderlings. A dozen more sanderlings are running and feeding in the surf, while out beyond them five herring-gulls rock gently on the sea. Two other gulls stand at the water's edge, and one is pecking vigorously at something in a pile of stranded sea-weed up the shore.

Full of peaceful bird life though it is, the scene seems incomplete without the oyster-catchers; but they have all flown off along the coast to mate and rear their young on a quiet stretch of sand, coarse grass, and shingle. The lone redshank has also left. I hope he finds a mate and company on some rough pasture, heath, or coastal marsh.

Head of Black-headed Gull
in breeding plumage.

And the black-headed gulls have gone, to rest and breed in close and quarrelsome community on some wild stretch of sand dunes, or a green tract of reeds and swampy grass, which soon will be resounding with their cries. Many of the gulls had patchy heads, and a few had even grown their chocolate masks last time I saw them. The sanderlings, turnstones and purple sandpipers can afford to linger a little longer before they fly north to meet the late Arctic spring.

It is now mid-afternoon, the tide has fallen, and I am walking down the shore between the rocks. I stoop to lift a large flint stone from the channel. I turn it carefully over in my hands to examine all its aspects, for it is an object of real beauty. Its surface has been painted with rich colours – green, blue-green, grey-green, ochre, yellow-green, yellow, and orange-yellow, intensified by patches of deep crimson and its own brown, untouched spaces.

The flint stone has been painted, not by dead, man-made pigments, but by the living sea. The colours are those of microscopic algae that settled on the flint stone, reproduced, and spread to form encrusting films around its surface. The crimson patches, like smears of new-spilt blood, are small, encrusting seaweeds, known by the scientific name of Hildenbrandia – they have no common one.

Further down the shore I lift a large chalk stone up on to its edge. Resting on the gravel below it is a young starfish about three inches across. I pick the starfish up and lower the stone back into place. The surface of the starfish feels rough and spiny. Its central disc and five arms are orange-brown, and at one side of the disc there is a tiny circular plate. This is the sieve plate and it is covered with microscopic pores which allow sea water to enter the starfish. On turning the starfish over, I see that its underside is yellowish-white. There is a mouth in the centre and along the mid-line of each arm there is a groove bordered by hundreds of little finger-like bodies which continually move in and out from the surface. These are the starfish's tube-feet. They are tipped with tiny suckers which enable the starfish to cling tightly to rocks or crawl about.

The starfish moves by using a water pressure system aided by muscles in its tube-feet. Water is drawn through the sieve plate into a circular tube from which two branches run the length of each arm. A double row of little bladders attached to each branch leads to the tube-

73

Young Starfish.

feet. When the bladders contract, water is forced into the tube-feet, causing them to extend. Muscles move the feet and their suckers grip the surface when they touch it. When the muscles contract, water is driven back into the bladders, and the feet are shortened, pulling the starfish forward. The suckers then release their hold and the action is repeated. In this way the hundreds of tube-feet working in unison enable the starfish to crawl smoothly along.

Now I place the starfish on its back on top of a flat stone in a shallow pool, and watch to see what happens. At first it lies still while its little tube-feet extend and wave about as if trying to find something to grip. Then the tips of two adjacent arms slowly start to twist sideways. The tube-feet also grope sideways and a group of them on one arm touches the stone surface. They immediately contract, pulling the arm further round and allowing more tube-feet to adhere. Meanwhile, some tube-feet on the adjacent arm have found a grip. A minute later the ends of the arms have righted themselves. Further down the arms more and more tube-feet grip the stone and thus pull the disc and the other three arms up and forward. Finally the starfish somersaults over, and now, with two arms leading, it glides slowly across the stone.

Chapter 12

The sea has covered the rocks and is lapping the cliff arms of the bay. About a hundred turnstones, twenty purple sandpipers, and ten sanderlings are resting on the beach. I see that some of the turnstones are coming into breeding plumage. These ones are tortoise-shell patterned to varying degrees, with orange-brown feathers on their backs, white patches on their heads and napes, and black marks on their chests. They will soon be flying on their long trek northwards, for in three days it will be May.

I expect you are wondering why it is that many birds change their plumage in the breeding season. At least, I hope you are, for the courtship and breeding behaviour of birds shows an elaboration and variety of gesture and colour that is unrivalled in the whole animal kingdom. Indeed, some of its performances are spectacles of such breath-taking beauty, that they might be described as masterpieces of natural pageantry. The subject is so vast, so little understood, and so wrought with wonder, that it seems impertinent, and rather presumptuous, to attempt a brief explanation. However, I shall just set forth a few ideas for you to ponder on, knowing that they raise a host of unanswered questions.

First of all, you should realise that in birds, the predominant sense is sight and that they see in colour, with hearing next, and smell an almost non-existent third. Thus, if a male bird wants to impress a female, he must make appeal to her eye, with displays of plumage and movement.

Breeding plumage is believed to have evolved together with acts and gestures of courtship. It is thought that the plumage colours and patterns which enhanced or emphasised the wearer's movements and postures, would increase their effectiveness in arousing the interest of his partner. Thus she would arrive more quickly at a state in which she could accept him, and co-operate in the act of mating. His plumage colours would then be passed on to the next generation, and so preserved, while less effective ones would not. In this way, colours which enhanced movements, and gestures which emphasised colours, worked together through the evolution of courtship – or so it is believed.

On the same basis, breeding colours would have evolved with gestures of threat among rival males, for it is in the breeding season that rivalry occurs. Thus, colour patches which served to emphasise these hostile gestures, and so increase their intimidating effect, would be preserved. In many species of bird these colour-enhanced threat gestures have, in fact, become powerful enough to eliminate the need for the birds to fight over a female, or in defence of a breeding territory, this, also, would be an advantage, for fighting can be damaging and wasteful of the species.

In many birds that co-operate in nesting and rearing their young, courtship and greeting gestures are performed between the pair throughout the breeding season. Now, if we follow the same line of thought, the plumage colours which enhance these gestures would serve to renew, and maintain, the bond of mutual attraction that holds the birds together. This would help them to co-operate faithfully in the arduous task of rearing their young, and thus increase their chance of doing so successfully.

However, many birds flock together on their feeding grounds during the winter months – turnstones and other shore birds, and black-headed gulls, for instance. At such times it is important that colours which might arouse hostility, or induce birds to separate in couples, should not be present – for safety lies in their keeping together as a group. Thus, in the case of these birds, the brighter, more provocative colours have become suppressed, and are reserved for the breeding season. Hence the change of plumage. On the other hand, the plumage of each kind must remain distinctive enough for the birds to recognise their own species.

Well, there are a few ideas for you to think about. Now it is your turn. Watch birds whenever you can, in films and in real life, with these ideas in your mind – and see how they fit in. You may find some broader explanations. I hope you do. At any rate, you will find joy – which is something much greater than pleasure. But now – back to the bay.

It is five hours later and I am walking along the beach. I stop and turn over some drying and rotting seaweed from the highest strand line. In doing so I surprise a host of sand-hoppers, which have only recently become active after sleeping deep in the sand during the winter months. They leap in all directions, then hurriedly scramble out of view below the seaweed and down into the sand. I replace their seaweed blanket and walk down shore to the rocky expanse.

Now I am walking warily with sudden jerks and lurches over its slippery, wrack-covered face. I give a mighty twist to save my balance as my gum boots skid into a crevice, and in doing so nearly rick my back. Ten yards further on, I bang down, clutching seaweed, as my gum boots go back-sliding on a mound. But it is worth a scramble to see the rock pools, for some are quite entrancing – like miniature gardens, planned and lovingly tended, in a breeze-rippled, glittering, underwater world. I crouch on my heels and gaze into one of these pools.

Wavy, transparent fans of green sea lettuce, half crumpled and tissue-thin, float outwards from its sides. Contrasting with these are the mauve-pink coralline seaweeds, growing in pale clumps, two inches below the surface. Their neatly branched and pastel-tinted

77

stems are all made up of many bead-like segments. I dip my hand and lightly hold a clump. Its branching stems feel hard and brittle between my fingers, for, like corals, they secrete a limy skeleton. Below the corallines, some dark green tassels of Cladophora, a filamentous sea-weed, fan out and upwards, like fine hair in the water. Green, curly ribbons of Enteromorpha, sun dappled and translucent, stream out-wards too, and below them are clumps of deep red seaweed, mossy, with multitudes of tiny, hair-thin branches.

Among the seaweeds are some gaudy flowers, but the flowers of this sea garden are really animals, called sea anemones. Each sea anemone has a broad and fleshy stem, or column. One is green and the other three are crimson. Circles of paler tentacles crown these columns giving each animal the appearance of a many-petalled flower. Inside

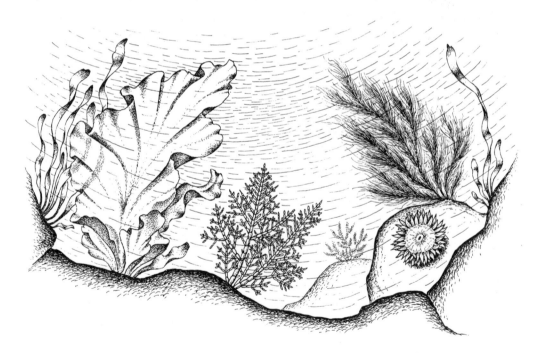

The edge of a Rock Pool.

the rings of tentacles there is a fleshy disc with a round mouth at its centre.

Very cautiously, I touch the centre of a sea anemone flower. Its tentacles close in and stick to my skin, while the mouth sucks at my finger as a young baby would. I pull my finger up from the sticky hold of the tentacles and at once the anemone contracts them into itself, closing the column above them so that it becomes a rounded blob on the rock.

I wait, but the anemone stays contracted. A small crab steps nervously out from the border of a stone, then scuttles across the floor of the pool and hides beneath a cushion of red seaweed. Now, two antennae, pale and faintly banded, wave slowly from the base of a Cladophora strand. They move out further, followed by four more feelers, a pointed snout, and two dark eyes on little stalks. The prawn comes fully out and floats down to the bottom, holding its long-armed little pincers out in front. The prawn walks smoothly with a gliding motion on three thin pairs of legs which barely touch the floor. Five pairs of swimmerets beat rhythmically below its abdomen, but the last pair, which is broad and flattened, turns back to form a tail-fin.

I gaze in wonder at the little creature. It is the loveliest of our crustaceans – a fair inhabitant for such a garden. Its clear, transparent body, decked with orange and violet stripes, seems to glisten with its own faint light. Daintily, it probes a tuft of seaweed with its pincers, then bends one pincer-arm and hands some morsel to its leg-like mouth-parts. These finger it in turn, then pass it upwards to the mouth. Now the prawn floats upward through the water, gently propelled by its beating swimmerets. I shift my weight to ease my aching knees, and like a flash the prawn has vanished. With a speed too rapid for the eye to follow it tail-flipped backwards to the green Cladophora strand.

Prawns can only be found on the shore in the warmer months. During the winter they live in the deeper waters out beyond it, but as the temperature rises in late spring they move shorewards again, to

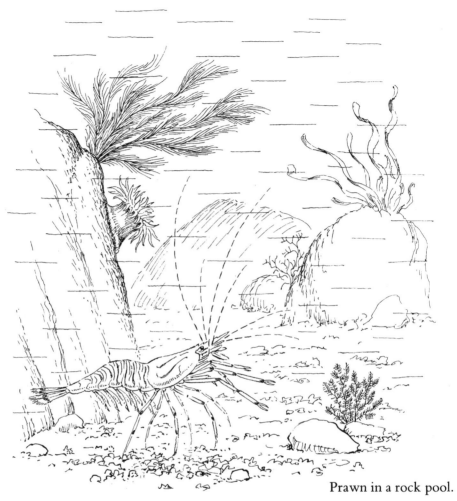

Prawn in a rock pool.

inhabit the various rock pools of the bay.

Shore crabs, porcelain crabs, gammarids, bristle worms, starfish, winkles, mussels, and many other creatures can be found throughout the year. In their abundance these go to feed the flocks of shore birds through the winter months. However, in the summer days that lie ahead, you will have the chance to find new creatures, which, like the common prawn, only make their appearance on the shore when the sun has warmed the sea.

SUMMER

Chapter 13

It is now the middle of May and I see that a pair of herring-gulls have nested on a ledge of the cliff face high above the bay. One of them – I do not know which, for they are both alike – is sitting on a mound of dark vegetation, incubating the eggs, while the other stands guard a couple of yards away. As I walk along the beach below them the gull standing guard gives harsh warning calls of 'ka-ka-kak, ka-ka-kak', which are repeated until it considers I have moved to a safe distance.

I stop and turn over some rotting seaweeds on the upper strand line.

Herring-gull nesting on the chalk cliff.

As the sand-hoppers leap away and disappear, I see that there are other small scavenging creatures living among them. Small beetles with long tails, like minute copies of the devil's coach-horse beetle, crawl over the newly exposed sand. Tiny black flies run here and there among the beetles. These little flies seem reluctant to take wing. Even when I pursue them with my finger, they run out of the way instead of flying. This reluctance to take wing is probably an adaptation that prevents them from being blown out to sea, or too far inland. I replace the seaweed over the community of little creatures and go further down the beach.

On the lower, wet strand line I find something that looks rather like a bunch of small, shiny-black grapes. This is the egg-cluster of a cuttlefish. The cuttlefish belongs to the class of molluscs which includes the octopus and the squid. Its mouth is surrounded by ten tentacles which bear sucker-discs, and it swims by means of an undulating fin on each side of its body, and also by expelling water through a funnel behind its head. The eggs, which are encased in black capsules with long stalks, are passed out through the funnel. As she lays them, the female cuttlefish entwines the eggs on some support, such as a stem of seaweed, and tangles the stalks of successive eggs so that they form bunches. As in this case, the bunches sometimes come adrift, especially in rough weather. I pick up the egg-cluster and feel the capsules. They are firm and not empty, so I take the cluster well down the shore, and wedge its stem firmly under a heavy stone. Now, perhaps the eggs will be able to survive and the baby cuttlefish eventually hatch.

A little further down shore I turn over a fair-sized flint stone. On the underside of it there are some barnacles, the twisty white tube of a Pomatoceros worm, the spreading growth of a polyzoan similar to the one I observed on the wrack frond, and a greenish sea-urchin with purple-tipped spines. The sea-urchin is clinging to the stone at the edge of the polyzoan, a portion of which has been more or less scraped away for a short distance around it – a pretty clear indication of what the

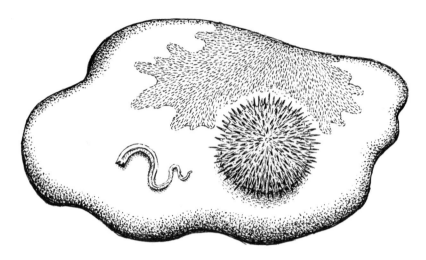

Sea Urchin on a flint stone.

urchin ate for its last meal.

The sea-urchin belongs to the same group of animals as the starfish, and like the latter, it clings and moves by means of tube-feet. Slowly and very carefully, to avoid tearing its delicate tube-feet, I ease the prickly urchin away from the stone. As I do so, its clinging tube-feet pull out well beyond its spines, and then release their hold and contract. Now I turn the sea-urchin over in my hand. At the centre of its under-surface I can see a circular mouth with five tiny white teeth, all pointing inwards, but protruding slightly, and meeting at their tips. These were used in scraping the polyzoan capsules from the stone.

As I pass above the herring-gull's nest on my way home along the cliff, I am not able to see the nest, but I can just see the guarding gull standing on the ledge. It turns its head up and sideways to look at me with one yellow eye, and repeats its clatter of alarm and warning. However, as I do not move away it soon loses nerve and flies out to sea, only to turn and fly straight towards me at eye-level height. Now it is I who feels slightly unnerved, but at about ten feet from me the gull veers off and out to sea again. Back it comes as I walk along the green, veering off as before and calling 'ka-ka-kak'. Then, satisfied that it has driven me away, it glides back to its ledge.

It is low tide, and I am down in a channel between the rocks not far from the sea's edge. There are no gammarids and few baby shore crabs in this region of the shore, but there are grey top shells on the underside of nearly every stone that I turn over. The bluntly conical shells of these little snails are closely patterned with narrow, dark grey or brownish stripes running obliquely from the apex down the sides. In some of the shells that I see, this pattern has been partly worn away, revealing the underlying mother-of-pearl tints that make them look very attractive. I pick one of the shells from a stone and turn it over. The little snail immediately retracts, closing the shell aperture with an orange operculum. The background colour of the shell is greenish grey with a touch of pink at the top, and the lines of its delicate pattern are slightly wavy.

I also find porcelain crabs on the underside of stones in this part of the shore. These squat little crabs – the largest are only a quarter of an inch across – have almost circular backs, longish, hair-thin antennae, and wide-elbowed pincer-claws that seem much too big for their bodies. Their claws are unequal, and in some of the crabs one claw – it might be the right or the left one – is more than twice as broad as the other, and looks quite a formidable instrument. However, porcelain crabs do not threaten you with their claws as a shore crab would when alarmed, or taken by surprise. They merely use them as an extra pair of legs to push with as they scurry backwards across the stone and vanish round its edge.

Porcelain crabs always run backwards when in a hurry to escape. They move on three pairs of outsprawled, slender legs, tipped with minute spines for gripping the stone surface. I pick up one of the little crabs to examine closer. It makes no attempt to use its claws in self-defence, but merely pushes feebly at my finger with them. Now, I see through my pocket lens, that there is a fourth pair of legs, but this pair is much reduced in size, and held forwards over the crab's back.

These tiny legs have probably shrunk and weakened through lack of use. Perhaps they are on the way out. It certainly looks as if the porce-

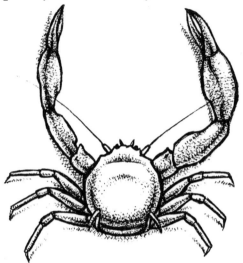

Porcelain Crab.

lain crabs are simply keeping them out of the way, having long ago decided that three pairs were enough. On the other hand, these legs could have some special, or occasional use, that requires them to be small and held over the crab's back. The answer lies in close observation. The problem is how to observe little crabs that spend most of their lives hidden away under stones of the lower shore.

I turn the porcelain crab over and see that, as in the shore crab, its tail is folded against the underside of its body. In this case, however, the tail completely covers the body and ends in a tail-fin. Now I drop the little crab into a pool. It floats down through the water, lands upside-down on top of a stone, and remains quite still in this position. Half a minute later it suddenly recovers from the shock of being handled, and swims clumsily backwards by making a series of forward flicks with its under-curved tail.

86

I am surprised to see this little performance, for the crabs never attempt to swim when I surprise them by overturning a stone under the water. Even when I touch or pursue them with my finger, they escape by running backwards – so I imagine that their tails are very seldom put to use. However, as the tail-fin has been retained, there may be occasions when the ability to swim, even clumsily, can help a little porcelain crab to survive.

I am now back home. There are three grey top shells on a stone in the transparent plastic tank that I have set up in my room as a sea water aquarium. I brought the top shells straight up from the shore, and now they are contentedly moving about scraping algae from the stone's surface. One of them is close to the side, and through the wide lens that I use for aquarium viewing I can see its pale, almost colourless foot, its short snout pressed to the stone, and the longish, slender tentacles extending from its head.

Grey Top Shell.

At the base of each tentacle there is a tiny black eye, and the tentacles themselves are greenish grey and neatly banded with dark lines to match the shell. As the little snail grazes the stone surface, its tentacles continually wave and rotate in a most lively manner. Their tips trace out invisible curves and circles, gracefully bending in the water as they move.

Chapter 14

It is a lovely June morning, just right for exploring the shore. I can see from the beach that the herring-gulls have two fluffy grey chicks in their nest on the cliff ledge. The heads and backs of the chicks are showing above the nest rim, in front of the standing parent gull. Its mate 'ka-ka-kak's' and swoops down over my head, so I move away

Sand-hoppers jumping away from my feet.

to the lower part of the beach. Here, as I stroll along, crowds of small sand-hoppers jump up from the wet sand in front of each step. The sand surface is pitted with myriads of small holes where they had dug their burrows. Looking up from the sand, I notice a dog-whelk on one of a cluster of mussels, fixed to a nearby rock. The dog-whelk is about the size of a large periwinkle, but less rounded. The shell is white with three broad bands of rusty brown, and it has a protruding notch at the front.

I pull the dog-whelk gently off the mussel. As I do so, it quickly draws in its yellowish foot, closing its shell with a brown-ringed, horny operculum. I am interested to see if the dog-whelk had been feeding on the mussel, but apparently it had not, for there is no tell-tale hole in the shell valve. The dog-whelk was, perhaps, waiting for the tide to rise and cover it, so that it could drill the mussel shell and begin its meal, protected by the water. On the other hand, it might simply have been using the mussel shell as a resting-place. In either case, the mussel is safe for the time being, for having retracted and closed its

Dog Whelk on a Mussel.

shell, the dog-whelk has no means of holding on. It would just fall to the ground if I tried to replace it on the mussel. However, as I like to interfere as little as possible with the life of the shore, I leave the dog-whelk below the mussels, at the base of the rock.

Dog-whelks are carnivorous sea-snails that feed largely on barnacles, but will also eat other molluscs, such as limpets and mussels. If I had left my dog-whelk on the mussel – assuming that it had come to feed – it would first rasp a hole through the hard shell valve with its sharp-toothed radula. The dog-whelk's radula is at the tip of a thin snout, or proboscis. Once the hole was drilled, the dog-whelk would extend its proboscis down into the body of its unfortunate victim, and rasp away the soft flesh as it sat contentedly on the shell.

One day, perhaps, it will be the dog-whelk's turn. A slender bill will grab it before it has time to retract into its shell. Another link will be formed in the food chain that contained it. A portion of energy that moved the radula of my dog-whelk will then, perhaps, sound in the piping call of a shore bird on the seaward rocks.

I step across a sandy pool, and some little gobies dart away and disappear as they spread their fins and settle, perfectly camouflaged on

Goby on the bed of a sandy pool.

the sandy bottom. These small, inshore fishes do not swim in mid-water, but move over the sand in sudden darts, like little underwater lizards, as they seek their prey. Further down I notice two more dog-whelks, one white and the other yellow, resting among a group of winkles, in a slight hollow on the side of a rock mound.

I pick an olive-green Idotea from a frond of wrack weed, and release it in a small pool in the channel. As it leaves my fingers, the Idotea appears to split in half, and two Idoteae, one smaller than the other, swim rapidly across the pool. I had picked up a male that was holding a female beneath its body – like some of the gammarids that scuttle away in pairs, when I lift up stones between the inshore rocks.

A few steps down the channel I move some wrack fronds and

90

expose a large shore crab, crouching in a gravelly hollow at the rock base. Instead of scurrying away, he lifts his claws and threatens me with open pincers. I cautiously lift him from the ground, and find that he too, is holding a smaller female clasped firmly between his front legs and underside. It seems to be in the nature of crustaceans that the female should be the smaller sex, and that the male should carry her about until her eggs are ripe and ready to be fertilized.

On my way upshore I see a red jelly-like blob on the side of a rock mound. This, of course, is a closed sea anemone waiting for the tide to

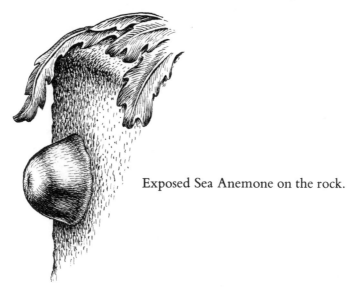

Exposed Sea Anemone on the rock.

return and cover it. A constant problem facing all creatures of the shore is how to retain enough water to breathe, and to avoid drying up when the tide uncovers them. They have solved this problem in various ways. Limpets and chitons pull down their shells flush with the rock. Periwinkles gum their shells lightly to the rock and draw in their opercula. Barnacles pull shut the little hinged plates that roof their shells. Pomatoceros and spirorbis worms plug the ends of their tube-shells with specially formed tentacles. Starfish, porcelain crabs, and grey top shells cling to the wet underside of stones. Gammarids

91

and little shore crabs hide in the puddled sand or gravel under stones. Flat winkles and Idoteae crawl below the fronds of damp wrack weed on the rocks. Large shore crabs retreat under big stones or wrack weed, or dig themselves backwards into the wet sand. Bristle-worms crawl into holes or narrow crevices in the rock, hide under stones, or burrow in the ground. But the soft and naked sea anemones, fixed to the side of rocks, must often endure long periods of exposure to sun and drying winds.

How, then, do they manage to survive?

In the spring I took a sea anemone from the shore, and kept it for some days in a small bowl of sea water. The anemone was closed up on an exposed rock and I removed it by sliding my penknife under the clinging foot, or disc, at the base of its column. Then, as I took hold of the anemone to put into a polythene bag, it expelled a large jet of sea water through its mouth by suddenly contracting. The sea anemone had now shrunk to half its original size, but in the water of my polythene bag it soon swelled up again. This performance had suggested an answer to the problem of its survival when left exposed on the shore. Before the ebbing tide uncovers it the sea anemone draws in its tentacles and closes up the column, with its stomach still full of water.

The body of a sea anemone could be likened to a sac with a small opening at the top which represents the mouth. The sides of the sac represent the column, the bottom represents the clinging disc, and the inside of the sac represents the stomach. The anemone closes the top of the column by contracting a ring of muscle just below its tentacles. This could be represented by a string threaded round the open end of the sac and pulled tight to close it.

Of course, the body of the anemone is far more complicated than this description suggests. The walls of its column consist of an outer skin, separated by a layer of jelly from an inner skin which forms the stomach lining. The stomach lining is drawn inwards in places to form vertical sheets running from the throat of the anemone down to its

92

base. These sheets separate the stomach into open compartments and greatly increase the surface for digesting its food. Vertical strips of muscle contract to make the column broad and squat, and encircling strips contract to make it tall and narrow. The tentacles of the anemone are hollow. It extends them by forcing water into them, much as you could extend the pushed-in fingers of a glove by blowing into the open end.

This brief account tells nothing of the complex network of nerves, the various senses, and the many different cells with separate functions, that enable the anemone to live. It is merely intended to show you the general body-plan, or bare architecture of the creature.

Now, to return to the sea anemone I brought home. I placed it on the bowl where it soon fixed itself and spread out its tentacles. I fed it

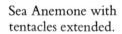
Sea Anemone with tentacles extended.

with a morsel of meat, for the sea anemone, despite its innocent and flower-like appearance, is a carnivorous animal. Its tentacles are armed with stinging cells that shoot out minute, barbed poison-darts into any creature brushing them. This enables them to hold and paralyse those small enough to eat. You will remember that when I touched an anemone in the rock pool its tentacles stuck lightly to my finger. This was due to the tiny darts they had shot into my skin which fortunately was too tough for their stings to penetrate.

My anemone grasped the meat with its tentacles, drew it towards the mouth, and sucked it in. Soon however – and I can fully sympathise –

it seemed to grow discontented with life in a small white bowl. It very slowly glided up the side of the bowl and the next morning it was half out of the water. I replaced the anemone on the bottom of the bowl, but the following morning it was fully out of the water. I left it there to see if it would go back of its own accord. It did not do so, and by the evening its skin appeared to be completely dry and of a dull brown colour. I touched this dry covering and found that it was loose, so I pulled it gently over the top of the anemone. It came off whole, like a jersey being pulled up over the head of a small boy – and there was the anemone, wet and shining, underneath. The film of fluid mucus which covers the anemone's body had thickened, and then hardened in the dry air of my room to form a protective water-retaining coat. The anemone had shown me its second line of defence against the danger of drying up.

Chapter 15

I have brought home three sea anemones and four little shore crabs to join the grey top shells in my aquarium. There are three stones in the aquarium – one chalk stone with green ribbons of Enteromorpha and a small sea lettuce growing on top, a small flint stone, also with a young growth of Enteromorpha and sea lettuce, and a larger flint stone covered with a film of algae and red blotches of Hildenbrandia.

You have to be rather careful about the kinds of seaweeds you put into a sea water aquarium. For instance, the wrack weeds quickly die, start decaying, and turn the water foul. Green seaweeds, however, seem to thrive. They not only decorate the aquarium, and give it a natural appearance, but also help to keep the water fresh. They do this by absorbing waste carbon-dioxide breathed out by the animal life and adding oxygen to the water in the daytime. Both animals and plants need oxygen to live, and must get rid of carbon-dioxide; but in the day, plants absorb carbon-dioxide, which they use in building food, and give off oxygen beyond their needs as a by-product of the process.

You have to be equally careful about the animals you put in the aquarium. Fishes and large shore crabs are too voracious and would eat up most of the smaller creatures. Large filter-feeding creatures such as mussels and piddocks, that draw a continuous flow of water through their gills, would soon finish off the floating microscopic organisms, or plankton, as they are called, and then they would starve. Large grazing molluscs, such as limpets, would quickly scrape away the small algae and other seaweeds from the stones, while periwinkles, being great wanderers, persist in climbing out of a small aquarium.

This sets a limit to the animal life that I can bring up from the shore for my aquarium, and excludes some of the more spectacular forms. However, this does not bother me, for all living creatures are unendingly fascinating. It would be stupid as well as cruel to stock the aquarium with creatures that could not live there for long. The important thing is that those I do keep should seem contented, and be able to survive in a healthy condition. Other creatures I bring home for short-term observation in a smaller container, and return them to the shore when I have finished.

Now I take the sea anemones from their polythene bag and place them on the larger flint stone in my aquarium. I space them out so that there is a large red anemone at one end of the stone, a medium sized red one at the other end and a small green one in the middle. They slowly fix themselves to the stone, but remain closed, and now I take the little shore crabs from the other bag and drop them in the water. There are three little crabs about a third of an inch wide, and a larger one,

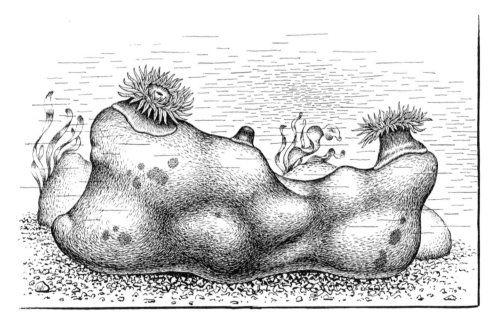

Sea Anemones in the aquarium.

96

roughly an inch in width. On reaching the floor of the aquarium they all scuttle out of sight under the stones.

Having given the crabs and sea anemones time to settle down, I bring up some tiny pieces of cooked meat from the kitchen. The two red anemones have spread their tentacles, so I give the large one a morsel, held at the tip of my forceps. As the meat touches one of its tentacles, those near it immediately bend over, like the fingers of a hand, and take it politely from me. Other tentacles now come into action, and all those surrounding the meat start to bend inwards, drawing it towards the mouth. Soon the meat begins to disappear down the anemone's gullet, and I feed the other one.

Now it is the shore crabs' turn. I drop four scraps of meat on the floor of the aquarium and wait for things to happen. A minute later a little crab comes out from under the chalk stone. It has scented the meat and starts feeling around with its claws, snapping them on shreds of seaweed on the bottom. Its searches gradually take it nearer the meat, and finally one of its feet touches a portion. Immediately the little crab pounces, covers the meat with its body, grips it with both claws, and scuttles back under the stone with its prize. In the meantime a second little crab has come out and started searching. It traces a devious path towards the meat, grabs a morsel, and runs back to the chalk stone. At the edge it almost bumps into the first crab, rushes up the side of the stone, and settles on the top to chew its meal in peace.

Now the larger crab emerges from below the small flint stone. This crab by-passes the two remaining scraps of meat and moves towards the chalk stone, where it scents the portions that the little crabs are chewing. It sidles up the chalk stone, sees the little crab on top and charges at it. The little fellow drops his meat, fairly hurtles across the stone, and hides underneath. The larger crab picks up the meat, moves off the chalk stone, and sidles back to his retreat.

Another minute passes before the third little crab comes out of hiding. It makes its way slowly towards the flint stone where the

97

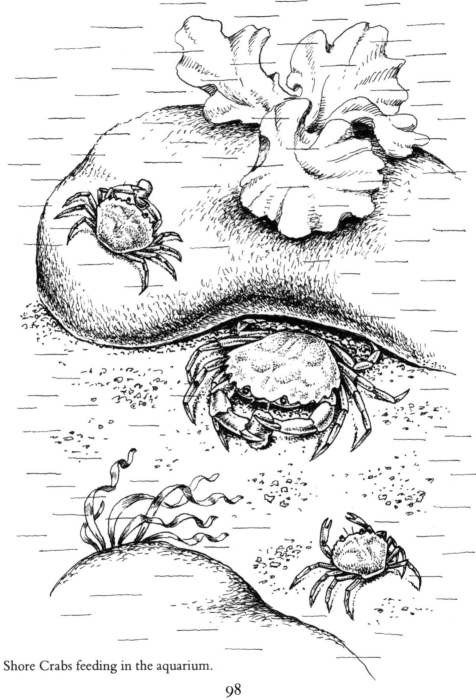

Shore Crabs feeding in the aquarium.

larger crab is feeding. Within half an inch of the stone it sees the larger crab and scuttles back in alarm. But the alarm is momentary, for the little crab comes straight out again. This time it moves towards the meat on the aquarium floor, searches around, and finally grabs its portion. Eventually the one that relinquished its meal discovers the last remaining piece. Now there are four young shore crabs contentedly chewing away, each with its portion of meat held firmly in both pincers.

Only the small green anemone is still without food, but it has begun to extend its tentacles, probably in response to the scent of meat diffusing through the water. I hand it a morsel on the end of my forceps and watch it slowly engulf its meal. Afterwards the meat still shows, as a pallid blur, within the green, translucent wall of the anemone.

It is a glorious summer morning. The July sun shines hotly on my face, and the sea, like a soft, and gently undulating mirror, tempts me to go in. I change into my bathing trunks on the beach, but I am not merely going for a swim. Before coming down to the bay I cut off the bottom end of an old nylon stocking, and fixed a little bottle in the toe by winding a rubber band tightly round its neck from the outside of the stocking. Then I made a loop of thick, flexible wire, twisted its two ends together with a pair of pliers, and fixed the cut, open end of the stocking to the loop with tough adhesive tape. I had constructed a small, makeshift plankton net for catching minute, floating organisms in the sea. I have brought the plankton net with me to the bay and also a jar with a screw-on top.

The tide is fairly high, covering all but the inshore rocks, and with my plankton net and jar held above the water, I wade down the wide, sandy gap. When the lapping wavelets have reached my chest I walk to and fro, trailing the plankton net just below the surface. Twice I stop to empty the contents of its little bottle into the opened jar. Now

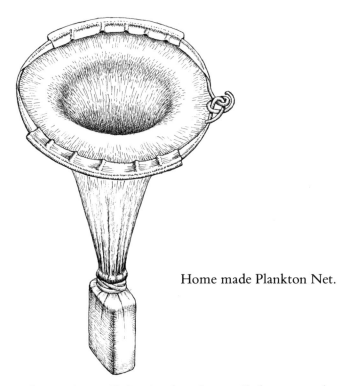

Home made Plankton Net.

I walk seawards, net in trail, jar in the air, until the water has reached my shoulders. Here I empty another plankton sample into the jar, trail my way back to low chest height, and collect the fourth sample. I repeat the performance, then walk up the beach, receiving a few interested looks from sand-lolling adults and sun-brown, jar-ogling children, who run up, but skip away on seeing nothing but water. I notice, however, that the water in the jar contains a slight, pinkish deposit, just under the surface.

I am now back in my room, and the jar is standing on my table. I take a narrow glass tube and with my fore-finger covering the top, lower it into the jar so that the other end is just under water. Now I lift my fore-finger to let a little water rise into the tube, close the top with my finger again to hold the water and lift the tube out of the jar. I take a microscope slide with a shallow cavity in the centre, and still holding the tube, I touch the cavity with it to release a drop of water.

I place the slide under my microscope and bring the water drop slowly into focus. As I do so, I see first the blurred, and then the sharply outlined forms of half a dozen transparent, glittering balloons slowly drifting in the water. At one end of each balloon there is a slight indentation with pale strands branching from it around the surface. Extending from the centre of this dip is a minute, transparent tentacle which slowly curls inward and then extends, or occasionally beats the water, causing the glittering balloon to revolve. These beautiful transparent balloons are single celled animals. They feed on the still smaller organisms of the drifting plankton, capturing these with the gently beating, sticky tentacle, which then transfers them to the mouth.

Noctiluca seen
through the microscope.

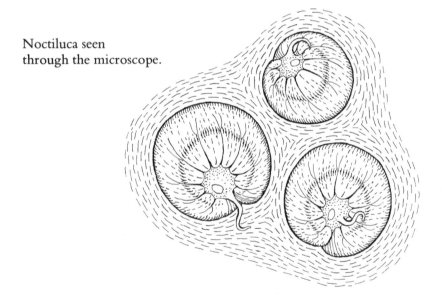

These tiny balloon-like organisms are slightly lighter than the water. They drift, in countless millions, just below the surface of the sea, and occasionally appear along the coast in summer. Their name is Noctiluca, which means 'night light', for they flash with brilliant light when the water is disturbed by breaking waves, or boats, or creatures swimming through them. There must be many thousands in my jar, and I wonder whether there will be enough of them in the sea for their lights to show up after dark. I shall certainly go and find out.

It is now nearly eleven o'clock. The soft, night air is cool and most refreshing to my skin, after the brilliant, sun hot summer day. The modest street lamps in the avenue high-light the leaves of dusky garden hedges, and spill green light-pools on the mown grass verges. Small moths dance and circle round the lamps, and occasional large moths gyrate with them, then hurtle off into the night. A pipistrelle bat flutters up the road, passes above my head, falls sharply, swerves, picks off a circling moth below the lamp, then flutters back head-high, its wing-webbed fingers flicking the faint light.

Now I step off the crunchy gravel of the road, and walk over the grassy stretch that muffles my footsteps to the cliff top. The sea is black as ink, but sheens with faint light in the middle distance. Small, dim-white breakers spill gently on the sand and utter long-drawn sighs before they vanish. Suddenly there is a flash of ghostly light, and then another, as small waves break above near-surface rocks. A faint light flickers further out then dies. Another faint light flickers on my left, and then two more. There is a pause – and now three brilliant green-blue flashes sparkle the water round the inshore rocks. Another pale light flickers on my left – and now the sea is dark, the night air still. I hear the sighing breakers crawling up the sand. A film of ice-green ghostlight forms, then fades in the black water. It is followed by three vivid inshore flashes. Two pale lights sparkle on my left again, where the offshore rocks are higher. A shimmering band of greenish fire moves over the midshore rocks, then dies. Two ghostly flickers break the darkness further out, and now a bright light forms, then flickers, dies, then reappears blue-green and brilliant, fades, then shines again, sparkles and spills itself along the inshore rocks.

The rhythmic sighing of breakers fades in the night air as I walk home over the dark grass. There were plenty of Noctiluca in the bay.

Chapter 16

There is only one chick in the herring-gulls' nest. I have no idea what happened to the other one, but this chick has grown amazingly fast. As it stands in the nest it looks about three-quarter the size of the guarding parent, which is perched above it on one of the concrete posts supporting the cliff top netting. I turn to go down shore and see the other parent flying in towards the cliff. It glides over my head and alights beside the nest. The chick at once makes frantic begging gestures. With head drawn in, beak upwards, it picks excitedly at the parent's bill, all the time making wheezy squeaks. The parent turns its head one way and the other and steps back trying to avoid the pestering chick, but suddenly gives in. It stretches its neck, points its open bill downwards, makes choking movements, flicks its head rapidly from side to side as if in the throws of a fit, then coughs up a large, wet glob

Herring-gull
about to feed her chick.

of food. The chick loses no time in gobbling this up while the parent gull flies off to forage for some more.

Down shore I turn over a chalk boulder lying in a corner joining the base of two rock mounds. Underneath it a shore crab is squatting in a watery hollow. I pick it up and discover that it is only the empty shell of a crab, but squatting below it is a larger, pale coloured shore crab. On lifting up this crab, I find that its shell is soft. The crab itself seems rather feeble in its movements and is barely able to struggle. I have discovered a crab that has just moulted its shell. Now I put the crab back in the wet hollow and look at the cast shell. I see that it is complete and undamaged, but has a neat slit along the back edge. This is where the moulting crab pulled itself out.

Once it has hardened, the shell of a crab, prawn, gammarid, sand-hopper or any other crustacean does not grow or stretch, and so has to be shed from time to time, like a coat or jacket that has become too tight. This allows the crustacean to grow larger in sudden stages, while its new shell is soft and can be stretched. When a crab is ready to moult it must first find a safe hiding place, for once moulted it will be entirely defenceless until its new shell has hardened. In preparation for moulting, substances in the crab's shell are re-absorbed for use in forming the new one. Meanwhile the crab's body starts imbibing water, and this causes it to swell until the carapace, which now has become rather brittle, splits along a line of weakness at the back. The crab then slowly struggles out backwards, and when free, continues to absorb water until its new, soft shell is stretched to the full. This will allow some growth to take place after the shell has hardened.

Having replaced the crab, its cast shell, and the covering boulder, I continue down shore. On the underside of a stone I find a young star-fish, not quite two inches across. I remove it carefully and drop it into a polythene bag to take home for my aquarium. Then I notice a winkle crawling across the gravelly bottom of a pool. There is something about the winkle that arrests my attention. It is moving in sudden little jerks instead of the smooth glide of a snail. I pick it up and find that it is no winkle at all, but a small hermit crab in a winkle's shell. The hermit crab has retracted and closed the shell aperture with an oper-culum – but the operculum is its right claw, larger than the left, and specially rounded to fit the shell. The hermit crab joins the starfish in my polythene bag.

The starfish and the hermit crab are now settled in my aquarium. When I left them the starfish had spread itself on the larger flint stone, and the hermit crab was peacefully squatting on the chalk stone, slowly waving its long antennae and alternately flicking the two antennules that protrude between its eyes.

It is a lovely summer evening and I could not resist coming out again

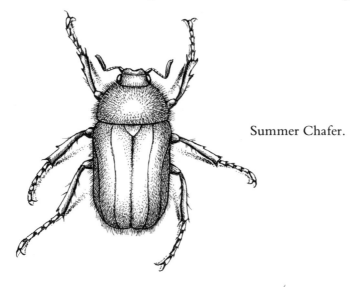

Summer Chafer.

to enjoy it. I am walking along the stretch of grass by the cliff top. The air is still, and the sky is pinky orange in the west. I stop and watch a summer chafer climb a stem, lift its yellowish brown wing-covers, spread its long flight wings, and take off with a dry buzzing sound. Another summer chafer flies past me, then two more. Now dozens of them are flying up from behind the netting on the cliff top where the black mustard, knapweed, prickly oxtongue, mallow, and bird's-foot trefoil adorn the uncut grasses. A few minutes ago there were no chafers to be seen. Now scores of them are in the air. They seem to know the exact minute when to wake up from their day-long slumber and take flight.

Suddenly the summer chafers start pursuing me. One settles on my neck, and I can feel its spiky legs. Another flies into my hair. Two more settle on my shoulder. Now there is a continued buzzing sound coming from the back of my collar. I bend back my arm and pick off a couple of chafers. They are clutching each other, but one breaks loose and flies away. Now I understand the cause of their interest and pursuit. The one in my hand is a female. I can tell by the smaller clubs on its antennae. Even as I hold it a male comes buzzing over my hand, so I place the female on a stem of knapweed by the netting.

I walk slowly back along the green, enjoying the thrilling sight of summer chafers zooming through the evening air and buzzing round settled females on the plant stems. Suddenly the peace is disturbed by a running, gesticulating man. He comes charging over the grass, waving his arms, ducking his head, and hitting out at the air as if pursued by seven demons. Of course I know the trouble. A female summer chafer has settled on his coat, and the demons are flying males. He thinks they are pursuing him and does not realise that their interest is only in a desirable lady of their kind.

The little crabs in my aquarium have really been rather naughty. They have snipped off all the fronds of Enteromorpha from the top of the chalk stone and left them lying about on the aquarium floor. However, thanks to their mischievous activities, I have discovered that other creatures actually live within the chalk stone. The other day, after the crabs had partly cleared the stone, I put tiny scraps of meat on it, for them to find. Before the crabs appeared I noticed that each scrap started moving slightly as if it were being jostled or pulled at from beneath by something very small.

Now that the crabs have laid bare the stone of all but a frond of sea lettuce, I am able to see what is visible of the creatures responsible for this. All that I actually see of each is a pair of extremely slender threads,

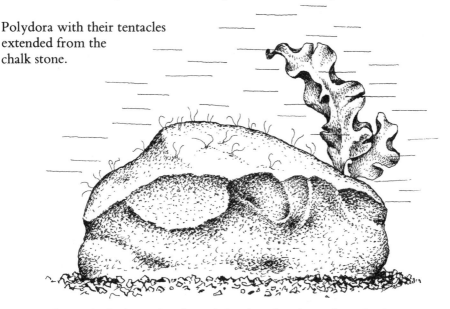

Polydora with their tentacles extended from the chalk stone.

waving and gently lashing back and forth. The threads, which emerge from a millimetre-wide hole, are the two tentacles of a minute worm, called Polydora, that has a tunnel in the chalk. The tentacles themselves, which are grooved down one side, are used for trapping microscopic organisms in the water. It is fascinating to watch, through my lens, this array of whitish, paired threads, all waving out of time, and each to its individual rhythm, above the surface of the chalk stone.

My flint stones also have their worm inhabitants. The small flint stone has two winding Pomatoceros tube-shells on its surface, and the larger stone has one. Each Pomatoceros worm has spread its funnel-shaped plume of tentacles, with its stopper tentacle, or operculum, curving to one side. The plume of the largest worm is dark red-brown, and those of the other two are pale and banded with dark lines. I dip my pencil into the aquarium and touch the plume of the largest worm with its point. Immediately the tentacles close and flash back into the tube with the end of the stopper covering them and closing the tube entrance. Half a minute later the stopper-end and brush of closed tentacles move cautiously out. Then the brush suddenly spreads to form a feathery crown, with the stopper pressed to the stone.

My hermit crab has taken up a more or less permanent station on top

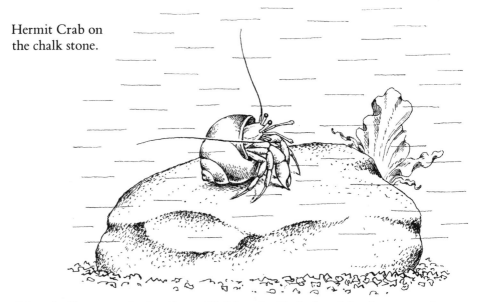

Hermit Crab on the chalk stone.

of the chalk stone. It sits there flicking its little knobbed antennules up and down, as if it were unceasingly tapping out mysterious morse code messages in the water. Meanwhile its stalked eyes stare out and slightly upwards from the edge of the winkle shell, and its long antennae occasionally wave or jerk upwards, as if scanning for other messages coming from afar. Really, the antennules test the water for the scent of food or enemies, and the long antennae respond to touch so that the hermit crab can move freely in the dark, and feel the stir of water caused by swimming fishes or other creatures moving near.

The hermit crab is content to rest fully exposed. It makes no attempt to hide away under the stones, like the little shore crabs. The bulky winkle shell on its back would, in any case, prevent it from doing so, but then it only needs to retract into the shell to be protected. If I walk suddenly up to the aquarium, the hermit crab retracts so quickly on seeing me, that it tumbles off the stone and has to climb laboriously up again, with the help of its claws and two pairs of walking legs. Its third and fourth pairs of walking legs are very small and are tucked away inside the winkle shell. They help to grip the sides, and its soft tail, or abdomen, ends in two small hooks which clutch the central column of the shell.

My starfish is very slowly gliding along the side of the aquarium near the surface of the water. I can see the little transparent tube-feet moving forward and down as it travels, millimetre by millimetre, along. How the starfish manages to organise these hundreds of little feet to work together on all its five, differently pointing arms, in such a way that it can move smoothly in a chosen direction, is very much of a mystery. I can see, through my lens, that there is a tiny red spot on the tip of the upward pointing arm. This is a very simple kind of eye, and there is one at the tip of each arm. These simple eyes enable the starfish to know whether it is moving towards the light or the dark, but that is about all, and it finds its prey by scent and touch.

The starfish is now moving up towards the smallest of my three grey top shells, which is resting on the aquarium side just below the water. As the leading arm of the starfish comes within a quarter of an inch from the top shell, the little snail suddenly wakes up and becomes aware of danger. It starts moving along, but the starfish's arm has reached the surface and it is trapped. Now the top shell struggles desperately to move out of the water and up the side of the aquarium. It pulls its shell right out of the water, but too late. A few of the starfish's tube-feet have fixed their sucker discs on to it, and the little snail is slowly dragged back into the water. More tube-feet fix on to its shell and the starfish glides over it until it is underneath the central disc. Now the starfish pulls itself into a hump and draws the top shell up towards its mouth.

Starfish eating a Top shell
on the side of the aquarium.

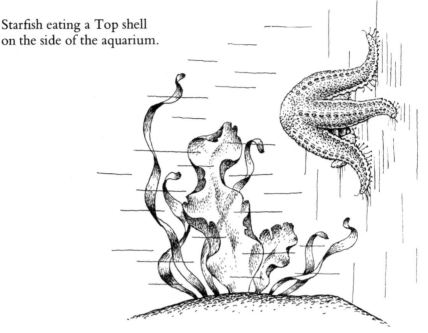

All day the starfish remains on the side of the aquarium with the top shell clutched to its mouth, between its up-drawn arms. The next morning it moves slowly down the side, drops the empty top shell on the aquarium floor, and glides away. It was rather sad to watch the fate of the little top shell, but at the same time it was interesting to observe the starfish's method of capturing and dealing with its prey. The starfish must live, and it is natural that an occasional grey top shell should become its victim. This top shell was unlucky because it happened to be at the surface of the water, and so could not escape easily when the starfish came along. I like to see the creatures in my aquarium pursuing their natural lives as they would do in a rock pool on the shore, even though it does mean that one occasionally becomes food for another. However, in the case of a rock pool, fresh animals are able to move in, and all are free to come and go, each time the flood tide covers it. As this cannot happen in my aquarium, I have to help out by giving the carnivorous creatures bits of meat.

I notice that the water level in my aquarium has fallen slightly, so I top it up to the right level with some fresh water. After I first poured in the sea water, I marked its level on the outside of the aquarium with a chinagraph pencil. This is the sort of pencil that will make marks on a shiny surface, such as glass or plastic. It can usually be obtained from shops that sell art materials.

It is most important to mark the surface level of a sea water aquarium and to keep it topped up with fresh water. The reason for this is that when the water evaporates, the sea salt is left behind so that the aquarium gets gradually more salty. This may kill the creatures living in it, for they can only survive healthily when the amount of salt in the water is the same as that in the sea.

I use water from the rain water tank in my conservatory for topping up my aquarium. Rain water is pure and much better to use than tap water, which may contain disinfectants and various minerals dissolved in it. Never top up the aquarium with sea water for then you are only increasing the amount of salt in it. When I come from the shore I do occasionally bring up a jar of sea water, but before pouring this into my aquarium I take out the same amount of water with another jar.

Chapter 17

August has come and the black-headed gulls are now back from their breeding ground. There were about seventy resting on the beach at high tide this morning, all looking very smart, for they still have their dark, chocolate brown hoods. Five equally smart oyster-catchers were standing near them. The herring-gull that guards the nest above the bay spends most of its time perched on a concrete post on the cliff top. It is having a very harrassed life at present, for people and children are constantly playing or walking on the grassy stretch by the cliff. The gull clatters harshly as they approach, then swoops above their heads

Parent Herring-gull on a post at the cliff edge above its nest.

as they pass. However, it is much more aggressive towards dogs than people. I saw it swoop down to within six inches of a large Alsatian dog, giving the animal such a fright that it ran off with its tail between its legs.

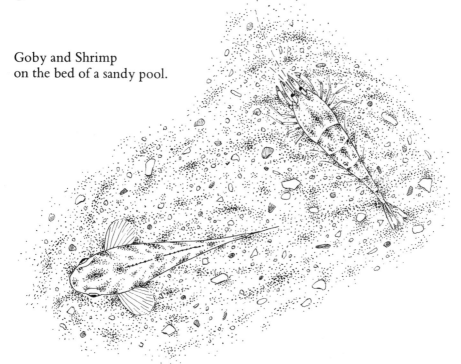

Goby and Shrimp
on the bed of a sandy pool.

The tide has now retreated and I am down on the shore. It is a warm, bright afternoon, and I am standing in a foot-deep, sandy pool by the green, inshore rocks. The little gobies that darted away as I approached the pool are now moving peacefully about over the bottom. They move in short jerks with a flick of the tail, then spread their round pectoral fins as they settle. Once settled, they are hard to see, for their pale, mottled bodies blend into the surrounding sand. Now I notice that a few are moving in a different way. They seem to glide along, and on looking closer, I see that these are not gobies, but shrimps. As I watch, one of the shrimps stops, and with a few quick shuffles, buries itself so that only its little stalked eyes and two long antennae are showing above the sand. I reach cautiously down, but before my finger touches it, the shrimp darts away leaving a little puff of sand that soon sinks back where it had been.

One of the gobies approaches my feet, then half swims, half climbs on to my canvas shoe. Another goby wriggles up and rests beside it, then snaps at my shoe lace and gives it a slight tug. Now a third goby swims up on to my shoe and chases the first one away. Meanwhile a half grown goby, only an inch in length, has swum and shuffled on to my other shoe. I look away from my feet and notice another shrimp burying itself in the sand. A nearby goby darts up and grabs at it – but it grabs a puff of sand, and at the same instant the shrimp re-appears a foot away. The shrimp had flipped backwards so fast that I could only see it suddenly take form, as if by magic, when it stopped.

I leave the shrimps and gobies and wander slowly down towards the sea. A large, dark coloured shore crab squats in a shallow puddle by the rocks. It lifts itself high on its legs as I approach, and turns to face me with raised, wide-open pincers. I bend down in front of the crab and move one hand behind it to lift it up. On turning the crab over in my hand, I see that the tail, firmly tucked against its orange-brown under-side, has the form of a narrow triangle. This shows that it is a male crab. The tail of the female is wider, and dome shaped, and she is generally much smaller than the male.

Now I turn the crab back-upwards and see that there are four

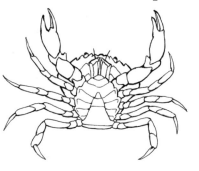

Underside of male shore crab showing triangular tail.

barnacles and a small, pink patch of Lithophyllum on its dark brown carapace. It must have taken quite a time for these organisms to grow, and they indicate that this is a fairly old crab which is no longer able to moult. I place the crab back in the puddle and it turns to face me again with upraised claws, not daunted by being handled and still full of fight.

Further down shore I notice a large starfish at the bottom of a pool. It is rather a fine specimen. The general dull yellow and orange-brown colour on the sides of its arms changes to red and then to mauve and blue along the tops. On lifting the starfish from the pool I am surprised to see a small, yellowish balloon protruding like bubble-gum from the starfish's mouth. The balloon soon deflates and is drawn back within the starfish. This was its stomach, which the starfish had extruded, probably while feeding. I search the pool for signs of its prey, but the water becomes so stirred up and muddy as I do so, that I am unable to find anything.

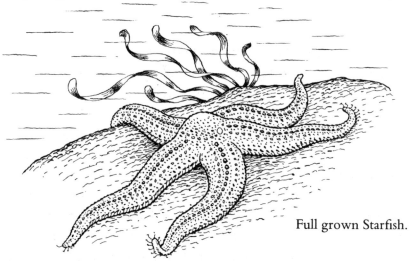

Full grown Starfish.

It is possible that the starfish had been feeding on some bivalve mollusc, and had extruded its stomach between the mollusc's shell valves in order to reach its flesh. Although the starfish has no teeth or jaws, it is quite capable of dealing with large bivalves, such as mussels, clams or oysters. If a starfish wishes to feed on a bivalve mollusc, it simply hunches itself over the shell and starts pulling outwards with its arms and tube-feet. Although the muscles holding the mollusc's shell valves closed are much more powerful than the pull exerted by the starfish, they tire more quickly. Eventually they start to weaken and a slit appears between the shell valves. Then the starfish forces its stomach inside-out through its mouth, inserts it into the slit, and pours digestive juices over the flesh of its victim. The mollusc's flesh is thus slowly dissolved, and absorbed through the stomach-lining into the body of the starfish.

The large starfish that I am holding has now become completely limp in my hand, and its colourful arms hang as if dead from my fingers. I place it under water at the edge of the pool and it immediately recovers. Its arms regain their former firmness, and the starfish starts gliding slowly away over the gravel.

I am walking along the green beside the cliff. It is a cool, early September afternoon, but bright and sunny. High water has passed and the sea is slowly retreating. Thirty turnstones and two oyster-catchers are resting on the sand of the bay.

I stop to watch a bar-tailed godwit fly in from the sea and settle left of the oyster-catchers. It looks an elegant and very distinctive bird, with its strikingly long, slightly up-tilted bill, slender back legs, and smallish feet. Now the godwit lifts its head and, with an air of prim delicacy, short-steps daintily over the sand, then stops to probe vigorously for food, half burying its bill in search for deeper prey. It works hard for its meals, mincing hurriedly from place to place between each bout of probing and thrusting in the sand. As if inspired by the godwit's activities, the two oyster-catchers move towards it, and also set themselves to probing in the sand. However, they do so in a more

Bar-tailed Godwit.

leisurely fashion, and soon give up.

The bar-tailed godwit is a winter migrant to our shores. It breeds close to the Arctic Circle in Scandinavia and Western Siberia, and nests on swampy ground, where there is a sheltering of scrub or scattered trees. This one must be among the first arrivals.

On returning from my long walk above the cliffs, I see that the tide has sunk far enough for me to enter the bay. Thousands and thousands of sand-hoppers leap up from the strand line and patter down like rain as I stroll along beside it. The sand below the strand line is pitted with their holes, and when I scrape it with my foot, more sand-hoppers climb out from the disturbed ruts and leap away. I see a glittering object on the sand ten yards in front of me. On coming closer I discover that it is a moon jellyfish, left stranded when the tide retreated.

The jellyfish is about eight inches across, and looks like a round, shallow dome of colourless, transparent jelly, except for the centre, where there are four violet, horseshoe-shaped arcs which give the creature a rather beautiful pattern. These are the reproductive bodies where sperms or eggs, according to whether the jellyfish is a male or female, are produced. I lift the jellyfish up, and as I do so, four fleshy, transparent lobes, fall and hang down from its centre. These are the mouth lobes, and they join up at their bases to form the central mouth. The moon jelly feeds on tiny animals of the plankton, which are trapped and paralysed by sting cells on the grooved, inner side of the lobes. These are then swept up to the mouth and stomach cavity, by microscopic, beating hairs, or cilia, that line the grooves. Food is finally transferred to all parts of the jellyfish in a current of water that flows through a system of fine canals. When I hold the moon jelly up against the light, I can see these food canals, like many transparent veins radiating outward from the centre to the rim of the dome, or bell, as it is called.

The moon jellyfish swims slowly by rhythmic contractions of its bell, but it is carried along by the currents of the sea. The best way to watch moon jellyfish, and to appreciate their beauty, is from the side of a small boat. One summer holiday I hired a rowing boat, and rowed myself through a shoal of moon jellies. It was a wonderful sight. There were hundreds of them gently pulsating along, just below the surface of the water. The violet pattern at their centres seemed to glow within the blue-sheened, pearly jelly of their drifting, softly thrusting bells.

The moon jellyfish belongs to the same big group, or Phylum, of animals as sea anemones and corals, and it actually has a larval stage that looks like a very minute, colourless anemone. This spends the winter fixed to rocks of the lower shore and beyond, then changes its form and finally divides into a number of tiny, star-shaped bells. These drift away in the sea and become baby jellyfish.

The stings of moon jellyfish, like those of the common sea anemone, are not strong enough to penetrate human skin, so it is quite safe to handle it, or to bathe and swim among them. However, there is another jellyfish, called Cyanea, that can give very nasty stings. This has a wide, yellowish-brown bell and yards of trailing tentacles. It occasionally drifts near the shore in late summer and autumn, and once, when I was swimming, head down, in the sea, I passed right over a big Cyanea. Its sticky, clinging tentacles trailed over my face and right down my body to my toes. If you can imagine what it would feel like to plunge full length into a thick bed of stinging nettles, with no more protection than a pair of bathing shorts, you will have some idea of the shock it gave me. I was living in a small caravan by the sea at the time,

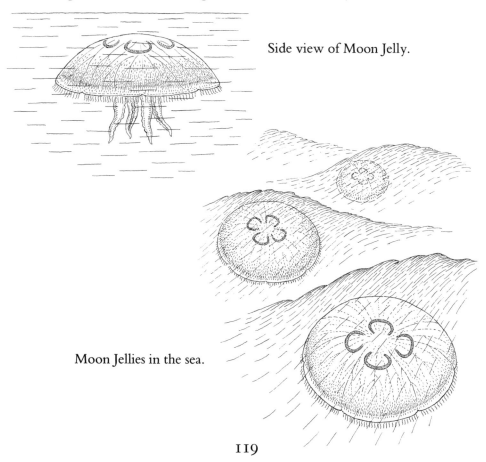

Side view of Moon Jelly.

Moon Jellies in the sea.

and there was nothing I could do but lie on my bed and endure the pain. However, after a couple of hours it had died away, and all I felt was a tingling sensation in my skin.

It would be unkind to leave my harmless moon jellyfish to dry up on the beach, so, not having my gum boots with me, I take off my shoes and socks, roll up my trousers, and carry it down to the sea. When I have waded as far as possible, I throw it out on to the shining water. On my way back I see another moon jelly, cast high and dry on the top of a rock mound, so I journey down shore again and throw it out to join the first one. I wish them luck, and hope that the receding tide will carry them far enough for safety. May they sheen and glitter in the sea, and go pulsating gently through the rest of their brief lives.

AUTUMN

Chapter 18

The spring tide has retreated far down the shore, and I am about half way between the inshore rocks and the sea. I lift a chalk stone from a shallow pool and a dark, eel-like fish darts out from beneath it and wriggles under some wrack fronds at the other end. I try to catch it in

Butterfish in a rock pool.

my hand but its slimy body slips quickly through my fingers. I want to make sure what kind it is, and pursue it across the pool. Now the fish wriggles out on to the gravel and I grasp it again, but it slips easily away and into the next, deeper pool. However, I manage to corner it, and force it back on to the gravel. Now is my chance – but again the fish slips through my grasp and back into the first pool.

I realise that it is hopeless trying to catch the fish in my hands and give up. However, it has swum out of the water, and is resting on some seaweed, under the rock ledge. It is five or six inches long, and its narrow body is greenish brown like the wrack weed, but the ten black spots, ringed with white, and evenly spaced along its back, identify it as a butterfish. Quite a good name – for it is as slippery as a piece of butter that has melted at the edges. If you can imagine trying to grasp a bar of wet soap that wriggles vigorously in your hands, you will realise how impossible it is to take hold of a butterfish.

Like the little gobies, the butterfish is an inhabitant of the shore, although it is usually found at a lower level. When the tide is out it hides under stones, or seaweed or in rock crevices, where it is fairly safe from gulls or other shore birds. Not being camouflaged to blend with sand or gravel like a goby, it avoids becoming stranded in an open pool that provides no cover. In fact, a butterfish will wriggle out of such a pool and push its way under a nearby stone, rather than risk being exposed to view at low tide.

Butterfish breed during the winter months. The eggs are laid in cavities of rock, old piddock holes, or the shells of bivalves such as mussels, but always under the cover of stones or seaweed. The female butterfish curls her body in a loop while laying her eggs so that they roll together into a ball, an inch or more across. When the eggs have been laid the male coils himself round them to protect them from being washed away. The female butterfish is reputed to relieve the male at times, so that they take turns in guarding the eggs during the month or so before they hatch. After hatching the fish larvae drift in the sea with the plankton until they have developed enough to start life on the shore.

Male gobies, and the males of several other shore fishes guard their eggs, but none of them show such close and intimate care as do the butterfish. Laboratory experiments have shown that there is a sound reason why the parent butterfish should take such trouble in holding the eggs together within the coils of its body. In some mysterious way, the eggs actually help each other to develop properly and hatch. When eggs were isolated from the batch in these experiments, they usually failed to hatch, and even if they did so the young fish were deformed. The reason for this is not understood at all.

I look up from the butterfish and notice a herring-gull on the rocks nearby. It is lifting strands of wrack weed in its bill and tossing them vigorously aside with up and outward sweeps of its head and neck, to expose creatures that were hidden underneath. The gull's action reminds me of the way blackbirds and thrushes toss dead leaves aside while searching for small creatures in the litter – but they do it in a crouching position, whereas the gull stands upright and throws the long strands high with outstretched neck. I turn and watch seven curlews fly over the sea, parallel to the shore. They settle on the far rocks to the right of the bay, where groups of oyster-catchers are piping and trilling noisily.

Now I walk down shore where the serrated wrack ceases to grow and the rocks are covered with carpets of red, mossy seaweed, only an inch or so in height. On looking closely, I see that scores of tiny midges, about two millimetres long, are whirling and pirouetting here and there over the wet carpet. They turn in curves and circles and figures of eight, running with open, vibrating wings, but never actually flying. When they come to a small pool, they stand on it and sail round and about, propelled by their vibrating wings. Many gnats and midges dance in the air in swarms, and these are perhaps performing a courtship dance on the seaweed. I am surprised to see tiny and fragile insects actually living on the lowest region of the shore, and wonder what will happen to them when the tide comes in.

Smooth, and rather fan-like, crimson fronds of dulse grow here and there on the mossy carpets, and the general red colour is relieved, in hollows and channels, by the vivid green of Enteromorpha and sea lettuce. It is surprising to see the green of the inshore rocks repeated down here. I have no idea what the complete explanation is, but it may be due, in part, to the fact that the green seaweeds of these rocks are no longer shaded out or smothered, by the more strongly growing, dark forests of wrack weed. Beyond these rocks, and in the sea-covered channels between them, the stems of large tangles stand up from the sea, with their long, brown, strap-like fronds falling around them, then spreading out and swaying in the water.

Still down on the lower shore, I lift a chalk stone, thick with ribbons of Enteromorpha on its surface, from a pool below one of the rock mounds. Leaving the stone on the red, mossy seaweed covering the rock mound, I look down into the pool and notice a dark, button-like disc with five writhing, snaky arms, pushing itself over the muddy sand. This is a brittle star, and I lift it out carefully to examine in my hand. Its hard central disc, the size of a shirt button, has five creamy

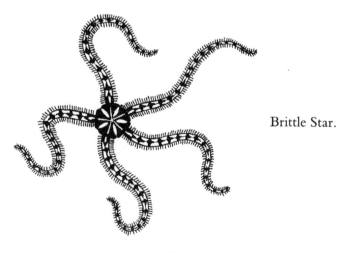

Brittle Star.

125

marks arranged in a star-shaped pattern on its surface. The narrow, tapering arms do not merge with the disc, as in the common starfish, but are clearly separate from it. They are prettily banded with green and grey, and edged on each side with short bristles.

The brittle star now starts to row itself over my hand by twisting and bending back two arms on each side, then bringing them forward again, while the front arm stretches then hooks back to help. To prevent it from falling off my hand, I pick up the brittle star, and immediately two of its arms snap off and drop into the pool. I see that they have broken off quite near the central disc, leaving little stubs; so I quickly replace the creature in the pool before any more damage is done. The brittle star is certainly well named. Back in the pool, the brittle star crawls over the muddy sand with the help of its other three, writhing arms, seeming none the worse for its strange and drastic behaviour. It will soon start to regenerate new arms.

Now I take up the chalk stone to put back in the pool, and as I do so a piece of Enteromorpha drops from it on to the rock mound. After replacing the stone I look up and notice, to my surprise, that the piece of Enteromorpha has moved away. Suddenly I see it pushing and leaping clumsily about further along the rock. I look closely and realise that what I thought was a bit of Enteromorpha is a little hump-backed prawn, three-quarters of an inch long, and the exact green of the seaweed.

This is a chameleon prawn, and before it has time to go back-flipping off the rock, I catch it and drop it into a polythene bag, part filled with water. After putting in a clump of Enteromorpha, I look, but can no longer find the little prawn. However, I know that it is safely in the bag, completely camouflaged among the Enteromorpha fronds.

I walk down a channel between the rocks where the sea flows in and splashes round my gum boots. Small creatures dart away in front of my boots, but they are difficult to see, so I stand still. Soon they begin to drift back through the water. Their bodies are quite transparent, but I can see their silvery antennae and their stalked, black eyes, moving like pairs of black dots below the surface. These are opossum shrimps, so called because the female carried her eggs and young in a brood pouch under her body. I bend down for a closer view, and they tail-flip backwards at lightning speed.

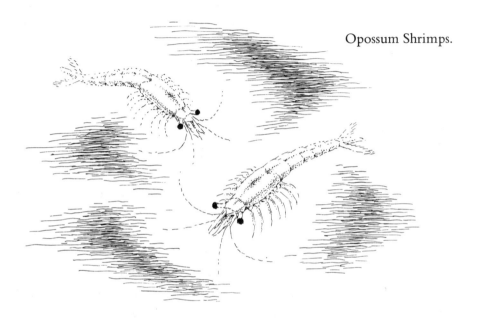

Opossum Shrimps.

I wait, and soon the pairs of black dots come drifting around my boots again. I can just make out the glassy forms of the little shrimps. They are about the same size as my chameleon prawn, but slimmer and less humped. They paddle smoothly along in nearly upright positions, using their eight pairs of rapidly beating swimming legs to do so, and to keep from sinking. Very slowly I lower both hands into the water, but the opossum shrimps dart away with invisible speed. Now I have my hands cupped under water, and wait for a little shrimp to come paddling above them. Soon there is one just above my hands and I jerk them up out of the water. The opossum shrimp jumps up and down in

127

my closed hands, but I succeed in dropping it into the polythene bag, which I had left open.

Opossum shrimps are quite unrelated to the shrimps that I saw in the sandy pool, or even to my little chameleon prawn that is similar in size and rather like them in general shape. In fact, opossum shrimps of one kind or another were swimming about in the ancient seas many millions of years before the true shrimps and prawns came into being. They belong to a group of crustaceans known as Mysids. Some kinds of mysids form dense shoals that swim in the open sea, and these are a very important source of food for ocean going fishes.

Higher up the channel, just beyond the inflow of the sea, I turn over a few stones. Little porcelain crabs hurry backwards to hide away as I do so. Most of the crabs are grey or light brown, but some are pure white, and I realise why they are called porcelain crabs. The smooth carapaces of these little white crabs do resemble bits of fine pottery. I turn up another stone and expose a young edible crab, about four inches across. Although bigger and more powerful than an adult shore crab, this young edible crab crouches timidly in the hollow, making no attempt to threaten me with its claws, or to use them in defence when I take hold of it. As I lift it up, the crab pushes its claws away under its body, folds and hunches its legs beneath it, and shams dead. The creature looks a really pathetic object, and when I put it on the ground it simply rolls from its hunched up legs and lands on its back. Now I ease my hand underneath the crab, still being careful to hold it in the safe way, and place it back-upwards in the hollow, where its legs are supported. Soon the young edible crab recovers from shock and unfolds its legs and claws, but still frightened by my presence, it squats back as deeply as it can into the hollow. I replace the sheltering stone and continue up the shore.

How different the behaviour of this young crab from that of the old warrior shore crab that I picked up to examine not long ago.

Young edible crabs inhabit the shore during the warmer months, but retreat to deeper water well before the winter comes. The fully grown adults, however, remain below the shore-line all the year, although they also move from deep to shallower water when the sea's temperature rises.

Edible Crab.

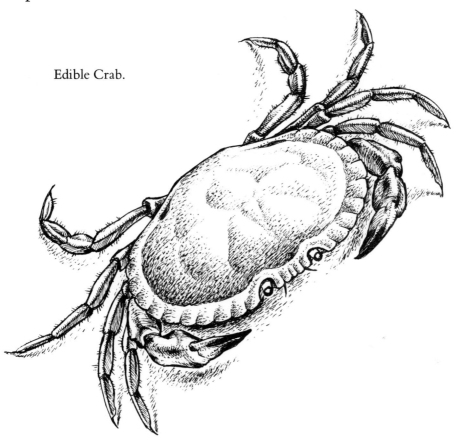

Chapter 19

Back home, I tip the contents of my polythene bag into the transparent plastic luncheon-box I use for viewing creatures in. This disturbance causes the chameleon prawn and opossum shrimp to shoot backwards, with forward flicks of their abdomens and tail-fins. However, after hitting the sides a few times, and jumping half out of the water, they settle down. The little prawn swims to the Enteromorpha clump and clutches a frond, and the opossum shrimp paddles slowly round in mid-water. Several times I return to my room to see how they are getting on, and each time I find the chameleon prawn clutching the

Chameleon Prawn.

same frond, while the opossum shrimp drifts like a little ghost, transparent and half upright in the water.

Before going to bed I take a last look at my luncheon-box aquarium. The chameleon prawn is now swimming in the water, gently propelled by the vibrating swimmerets below its abdomen. The little creature is no longer green, however. It has become a pale, translucent blue colour, and seems nearly as unsubstantial as the opossum shrimp. This marvellous ability to lose its opaque colour helps to protect the prawn while it is active in the night. There is no point in the prawn being green at night time, when colour no longer shows. In any case, its movements would give it away to whatever hungry fish might come along – so it becomes translucent blue and merges with the water. Then, when the dawn light touches the surface of the sea, the little prawn settles to rest in a clump of Enteromorpha, regains its green colour, and merges with the fronds.

In the morning I look for the chameleon prawn, and at last make out its form, green as ever, among the Enteromorpha ribbons. The opossum shrimp is half resting with its tail-fin on the bottom. It seems lethargic, and when I touch the little creature it tail-flicks up, but slowly sinks again. The confinement is doing it no good. These two crustaceans feed by sifting minute creatures from the water current, drawn across their mouth-parts by rapidly-beating legs or small appendages. They would not survive for long in my aquarium, so I pour them back into the polythene bag, tie it up, and make my way down to the shore.

After releasing the two crustaceans in the sea, I wander about the lower shore. Suddenly I notice a small red prawn swimming above some strands of red, hair-like seaweed in a deepish pool. With cupped hands, I succeed in catching the little prawn and pop it into the polythene bag with some water and a few strands of the seaweed. On looking closely at the creature through the side of the bag, I see that it is another chameleon prawn, differing only in colour from the last.

Having lived among red seaweed, this prawn had taken on its redness. Green is no more a natural colour for the chameleon prawn than red, or perhaps brown. What is natural to it, is the ability to merge in colour with the kind of seaweed that it rests on in the day.

On my way up shore I turn over a few stones, and under one I find a slug-like creature, fixed to the surface in a humped position. It looks like an ordinary pale-grey field slug, but feels softer to the touch. I take the stone and place it in a nearby pool. As the water covers it, the creature's back fluffs out into a coat of small, tentacle-like bodies called cerata. Now I recognise it as a young specimen of the grey sea slug. While I watch, the sea slug stretches out, causing the cerata to part along the mid-line of its back. The head, with two extended tentacles protrudes, and the slug starts gliding slowly forward. I shall

Grey Sea Slug.

not take the grey sea slug home for my aquarium, for it feeds on sea anemones, so I make a sketch of it to take home instead.

There are two very remarkable facts about the grey sea slug. The first is that it is able to eat sea anemones without being paralysed or killed by their stings. The reason for this is that, in some mysterious way, the sea slug is able to prevent the anemone's sting cells from discharging their poison darts. The second remarkable fact is that the anemone's sting cells are not digested, along with the rest of its body, by the sea slug. Instead, they pass unharmed from its stomach, and travel into the fleshy cerata that cover the sea slug's back. They are stored in these cerata which somewhat resemble a sea anemone's tentacles, and are used to defend the slug itself. Thus armoured with the weapons of its prey, the grey sea slug will discharge these sting cells into the mouth of any creature misguided enough to try and eat it.

Back in my room I empty the water with the red prawn and red seaweed into my luncheon-box, but before the prawn settles, I catch it and put it in a little cup of sea water. Now I push the red seaweed to one end of the luncheon-box, and place some green Enteromorpha at the other end. Will the chameleon prawn choose the right seaweed to settle on? I lower the cup into the water and let the prawn swim out. After swimming round for half a minute it settles on the red seaweed. I repeat the experiment several times, and on each occasion the chameleon prawn settles on the red seaweed. It is able to recognise the seaweed that corresponds to its body colour, and makes a deliberate choice of that seaweed for resting on. As the chameleon prawn is unable to change its daytime colour quickly, it is vital that it should recognise the seaweed on which its body will merge. Were it to choose the wrong one, it would show up in vivid contrast, with a high chance of being eaten before the few days elapsed in which it could make the colour-change.

It is a bright October morning, but there is a cold breeze blowing inland. The sea is cobalt blue and choppy, with foaming breakers tumbling on the beach. A hundred oyster-catchers and two herring-gulls are resting on the sand. About thirty turnstones are trotting here and there, searching for food among the piles of stranded seaweed. A curlew and a redshank wander about stopping to jab their bills into the sand; and a party of sanderlings are alternately chasing the dying breakers and being chased up-shore by the next line of frolicking surf. Five black-headed gulls – their heads now white because the breeding season is over – are searching for scraps at the water's edge, and six others are tossing up and down as they float on the dancing sea.

The breeze died down at mid-day, and now, in the late afternoon, it is calm and peaceful on the lower shore. I lift some wrack fronds that hang from a rock mound, and uncover a spider crab, resting in a hollow at its base. The crab is about one and a quarter inches long. Its body has the form of a slim triangle with a pair of small, short-stemmed eyes at the pointed, front end. It looks, and feels, like a rather fanciful

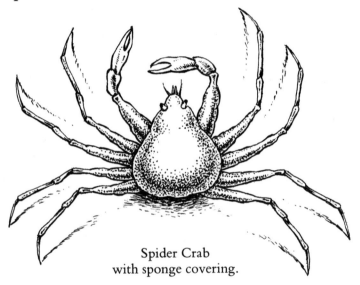

Spider Crab
with sponge covering.

toy crab, made of rubber, for its carapace, its narrow claws and its long, spidery legs are covered with a pelt of yellowish fawn sponge. This close-fitting sponge jersey serves to protect the crab, for sponges are highly distasteful to most creatures. The spider crab is timid and slow moving, but its amazingly flexible claws reach backwards over its carapace and probe at my fingers while I hold it.

There is a special reason for this flexibility, which allows the spider crab's claws to reach over its back. The sponge jersey did not just happen to grow on the crab's back, it was actually placed there by the spider crab itself. At least, the spider crab started it off by nipping bits of sponge from the rock surface, and placing them on its carapace and legs. There are minute tubercles on the crab's body which hold these bits of sponge in place. Soon they start to grow and spread over the spider crab, thus protecting it from predators.

This purposive action of the spider crab in placing snippets of sponge on its back suggests a fairly high order of intelligence. However, it is an instinctive, and not a learned action. The spider crab is born with the need to cover its body. I do not suppose it has any idea why it does so, although the crab probably experiences a sense of being naked or insecure without a covering.

To me, the fact that the spider crab's action is not intelligent, in no way diminishes the marvel of its behaviour. The instincts which enable creatures to survive and carry out their complicated actions are enthralling mysteries, which make their study always so exciting. However, not wishing to annoy this strange and delightful little being in my hand – which makes me think of a daddy-long-legs in a life-jacket – I replace it in the hollow below the wrack fronds.

Now I turn over a large chalk stone in a shallow pool between the rocks. A dull green creature with long, forward-pointing claws, runs rapidly backwards over the stone, in just the same manner as the porcelain crabs did. I make a grab for it, but the creature shoots back-wards to the other end of the pool. Here I catch it. I can feel its tail vibrating rapidly in my hand as it attempts to swim away, so I drop it in the polythene bag. It is about one and a half inches long, with narrow claws, nearly as long as its body and it looks like a little green lobster with its tail tucked underneath it.

The creature is called a squat lobster, but it is closely related to the porcelain crabs, and like them it runs backwards on three pairs of walking legs when escaping. I take the squat lobster out of the bag and hold it upside-down. Its fourth pair of legs is now visible. They are

135

small and slender and are tucked against its body. Like those of porcelain crabs they appear to be quite useless. The tail-fin is well developed, and as I hold the creature its abdomen uncurls and then beats forward in a series of rapid vibrations. It makes no attempt to nip me with its long pincers, but merely struggles to escape. Back in the pool, the squat lobster tail-flips backwards, shooting itself half out of the water then settles on the bottom. I replace the chalk stone, and it scuttles backwards and retreats beneath it. Soon it will retreat still further, to spend the colder months in deeper water, safe from the probing bills of hungry shore birds.

Squat lobsters of this kind do not use their claws for catching prey. They feed on organic particles and minute creatures, which are swept into their mouths by vibrating, hair fringed mouth-parts. For this reason they would not survive in my aquarium.

Before leaving the shore I pick up an empty dog-whelk shell, nicely marked with brown and white bands. I want to see how my hermit crab will react to it.

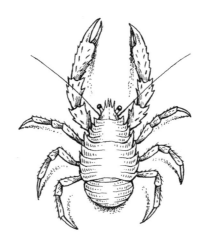

Squat Lobster.

Chapter 20

I have placed the dog-whelk shell in the aquarium, and on the chalk stone near to where my hermit crab is squatting. The crab shows immediate, but cautious interest. It goes up and touches the shell with its antennae, and then moves nearer and pokes a claw into the shell aperture. Now it cautiously grips the edge of the shell with its other claw. This causes the shell to rock forwards, and the startled hermit

Hermit Crab in
the Dog Whelk shell.

crab jerks back into its own shell so quickly that it rolls off the stone with a clatter. However, the crab scrambles up on to the stone again and goes straight over to re-inspect the shell. This time it pokes its front legs and both claws into the shell and feels around inside it.

Satisfied, at last, that the shell conceals no dangerous inhabitant, the hermit crab reaches up and grasps the top edge of the aperture, lifts its front legs on to the shell and pulls itself over it. This causes it to extend far out from the winkle shell. It frees itself from the latter, and for a fraction of a second I see the crab's rather worm-like tail with the little hooked limbs at the end, as it flips out of the winkle shell, which rolls backwards. I have that brief glance only, for in all haste the hermit crab curls its tail beneath it and thrusts it up into the new shell. The creature acts as if it were well aware that its soft, unprotected tail, or abdomen, would be a tempting morsel for a fish, a shore crab, a gull, or any other predator that came along.

The hermit crab now has a more roomy, though heavier shell, which will allow it to continue growing for some time. The nicely banded dog-whelk shell has made it a much more decorative inhabitant of my aquarium than formerly. Maybe the hermit crab was glad to get rid of the old grey winkle shell, but it was concerned with comfort not appearances.

The hermit crab and its shell provides a very interesting example of a link between a crustacean and various kinds of gastropod molluscs or sea-snails. Earlier in the book I mentioned how the creatures of the bay were linked together by their different feeding habits to form a food web where all were dependent, in one way or another, on other animals and on the plants. In the case of the hermit crab and its shell, however, we have a link between two animals which has nothing directly to do with eating or being eaten.

Although winkles and dog-whelks are not living partners of the hermit crab, the creature none the less depends on their ability to produce shells, a few of which will later be used for its protection. In other words, the hermit crab, having lost the ability to secrete a skeleton around its abdomen, borrows the shell, or skeleton, of a sea-snail which, being dead, has no further use for it. There is a very interesting case of a land-living hermit crab in Bermuda which uses the shells of a snail that has become extinct. This means that it relies, for protection, on the past shell-making activities of a snail that is no longer in existence.

My hermit crab accepts scraps of meat just as readily as the young shore crabs do. When I drop a morsel of meat behind its shell the crab quickly scents it, swivels round, and moves over to grab it up with a pincer. Its method of taking the meat is quite different from that of a shore crab. The shore crab holds the meat in front of its mouth between its two horizontally held claws, which have their elbow-joints pointing out sideways. The hermit crab takes the meat with its claws pointing down and backwards and the elbow-joints pushed out in front of its head. Then holding the meat beneath it, with its large claw, it pulls bits off with its smaller one and lifts them to its mouth. Later the crab holds the meat up to its mouth, supported by both back-pointing pincers.

Shore Crab
eating a bit of meat.

While watching the hermit crab I noticed that Pomatoceros worms are sensitive to daylight, and respond to a shadow moving across them by drawing in their tentacles. I happened to see the largest of my Pomatoceros worms pop back into its tube-shell when I moved an arm between it and the window. Its reddish brown funnel of tentacles soon moved out again, so I repeated the action and it shot back into the tube. I have tested this response many times since.

The Pomatoceros has no eyes, so the tentacles themselves must be able to sense a shadow moving across them. This sensitiveness to shadows must help in the survival of these worms, for it would prevent an inquisitive fish or crab from nipping off their heads. Strangely enough, my Pomatoceros worms do not respond in electric light. I can move my hand across the lamp and cast a shadow over them dozens of times, but their little crowns of tentacles do not move.

My sea anemones reveal their animal nature by their constant movement, although it is usually too slow to perceive with the naked eye. A couple of days after I put them into the aquarium, the medium-sized red anemone disappeared out of sight under the flint stone. Later, it glided out again onto the top of the stone. Meanwhile the large anemone had moved from the top down to the side. I never know quite where I shall find them from day to day. The little green anemone seemed contented to remain on one small area of the stone for weeks – then one morning I found it on the side of the aquarium. The next day it had moved round the corner onto the other side – a distance of over six inches.

The sea anemones not only move, they are continually changing their shapes. One day all will be extended, displaying their coronas of

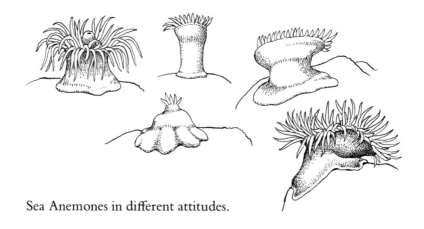

Sea Anemones in different attitudes.

tentacles. The next day one, two, or all, will have retracted to blobs of jelly. Sometimes their columns, whether their tentacles are extended or not, will be tall. Another day one or two may have spread themselves into wide flattened forms. A closed anemone may have a rather pointed shape one day, and a smoothly rounded shape the next, or its column may be slightly pinched in at one part and bulging at another. There is continual interest in seeing how they have moved, or changed

140

their shapes, even though I cannot actually observe them doing so.

About six weeks after I put him in, the larger shore crab in my aquarium captured and ate one of the smaller crabs, just after it had moulted, and while it was in a soft and helpless condition – so I returned the other two small crabs to the shore. Now the larger crab has moulted himself, and has increased in width by about a quarter. When I first had him – the crab is a male – he was so timid that he would scuttle under a stone whenever I came near, or even when I turned the page of a book, as I sat at my table by the aquarium.

Now, however, he has become quite tame. If hungry, he comes to the side of the aquarium when I approach it. When I drop a bit of food in the water he tries to kick his way up to the surface to grab it before it sinks. He even climbs to the top of a stone and greets me with claws raised in readiness when I put my hand over the water, and jumps up if I dip my finger in. He seems to have learnt that my hand is a provider of food.

When you consider that the crab is a Crustacean, like a woodlouse or a shrimp, and that he belongs to the large animal phylum 'Arthropoda', which includes insects, spiders, and centipedes, it seems remarkable that he should have learnt so quickly.

Chapter 21

It is not cold for mid-November, but there is a blustering west wind with intermittent squalls of lashing rain. The sky is grey and yellow-grey and purple, and dark-toned, ragged shreds of cloud race and scurry eastwards below the paler ceiling. The sea has a more opaque and leaden greyness, with rolling patches of white foam above the higher, submerged rocks, right of the bay. Its brown-grey edges, thick with suspended sand, tumble in white breakers that spill in creeping, sud-flecked tongues along the beach.

Quick sketch of Sanderling.

Below where I stand on the cliff top, a compact group of seventy resting sanderlings makes an almost perfect, solid circle. Its brownish, wet-sand base is closely and evenly specked with the plump, silvery grey bodies of the birds. Near the disc of sanderlings, six oyster-catchers are resting, and to their left along the beach, there are a dozen more. Near the oyster-catchers are three herring-gulls. Two of the herring-gulls are hunched in sleep, but the other stands stiffly upright while, with down-curved neck and in-pointing yellow bill, it nibbles and preens its white, out-jutting breast. Beyond the herring-gulls, a few turnstones and two black-headed gulls are probing and pecking among the piles of sodden seaweed.

I start to walk along the cliff and immediately the flock of sanderlings flies out to sea. It forms a flat and glittering cloud of close-packed birds that shoots over the water followed by the six oyster-catchers. The cloud elongates and gleams white with the bellies of its bird components as it curves, then broadens again to a flat, fast-twinkling oval as it comes speeding inland. Above the beach the cloud disintegrates, and seventy fluttering birds alight upon the sand. Meanwhile, the six oyster-catchers continue on their course above the sea and disappear beyond the jutting cliff.

The damp, westerly air stream has brought out the little striped snails. All along the cliff top they are there in their many thousands, moving along the leaves, and up the stems, and over the seed-pods on

Striped Snail.

the seaward side of the netting. Here, the yellows and browns and greens and bleached straw colours of the wet and tangled forest of grasses and dying herbs and seed heads, gives them nourishment and exercise and shelter.

These are attractive little snails that cling to the cliff top, and do not mind a sprinkle of sea salt with their food. Each plumply disc-shaped shell, a quarter to half an inch across, and white or creamy pale, is decorated with a single dark brown band. This runs along the mid-line of the shell and follows the curling whorls up to the last tiny coil of its flattened apex.

The little striped snails are not seen in spring, for they are then hibernating in the soil among the grass roots. They are creatures of late summer and damp autumn days. They feed on the late greens and the decaying vegetation, until the threat of winter sends them in retreat to sleep among the roots and rhizomes of the shallow soil above the chalk.

On returning from my walk along the cliff top, I see that a number of black-headed gulls have settled on the green above the bay. Among them are a few slightly taller gulls of much the same size. They resemble the larger herring-gulls in general body colour, but have dark eyes, yellowish green, more narrow bills, and dull green legs. I realise, to my delight and surprise that they are common gulls. The common gulls do not breed in England. They are winter visitors to the south, and spend the spring and summer months around their breeding grounds on freshwater islands or grassy moorland sites surrounding lochs in Scotland and Northern Ireland.

I notice that one of the common gulls is performing a peculiar standing dance. It is beating its feet rapidly up and down on the same little patch of grass. Every half minute or so the gull stops and cranes its neck to one side or the other as if looking for something on the ground, then repeats its on-the-spot dance. Now it stops, cranes its neck to one side, then bends over, pulls up a worm, and gulps it down. At once the gull starts padding its feet up and down again, turning its head one way and the other as it does so. Suddenly it stops, swivels right round, and pulls up another worm from behind it. It then recommences its foot-beating activity.

The common gull is tapping the ground to bring up earthworms. Fascinated by the performance, I watch the gull for a full ten minutes. During that time it collects eight worms, three large, and five about half grown from the one small patch of ground. The gull has discovered a very successful way of finding worms. I should never have thought that there could have been so many living below a square foot or so of grass.

Common Gull
foot-tapping for worms.

I wonder if the common gull had recognised some outward sign that indicated there were worms below that patch of ground, or whether it was just lucky and had picked the patch at random. It would be most interesting to find out whether or not the ground for foot tapping is consciously selected by a gull. I think it very likely that it is, and that the gull learns to interpret signs, worm casts for instance,

145

or more subtle ones, and knows where its activities will yield results and not be wasted. After all, blackbirds and thrushes on the lawn know where worms they cannot see are lurking just below the ground. A half-hour by the window will tell you that.

The cold east wind whips the sea into foam-capped waves, and sends the herring-gulls up into the sky to lean with outstretched wings upon its forces. Winter has returned to the bay.

My happy hours spent among the rock mounds of its shore, and on the cliff that bounds it, were filled with marvelling at the resilience of its varied creature-forms that manage, in so many different ways, to survive the storms and pounding breakers that beset it, and adjust their life-styles to the flood and ebbing of its waters. Some of the bay's inhabitants are strongly or heavily armoured, others are fragile and most delicately made, yet all show equal toughness in meeting the demands and special problems that the sea-shore offers.

I have described to you these happy hours among the creatures of the bay. I have attempted to convey my sense of wonder and, at times, of awe, at the beauty, power, fragility, or strangeness of its sentient beings, whose world is so remote and different from ours. I hope that you enjoyed the telling. I hope, too, that your all-too-quickly-passing holidays at the sea-side will be enhanced by an awareness of its living marvels. My wish is that they may give you so much pleasure that you will become concerned about preserving, in all its splendour, this life-rich and exciting ecosystem, and in keeping it intact and undefiled.

Index